National Children's Bureau series

Editor: Mia Kellmer Pringle

This new series examines contemporary issues relating to the development of children and their needs in the family, school and society. Based on recent research and taking account of current practice, it also discusses policy implications for the education, health and social services. The series is relevant not only for professional workers, administrators, researchers and students but also for parents and those involved in self-help movements and consumer groups.

Caring for Separated Children
R. A. Parker (editor)

A Fairer Future for Children
Mia Kellmer Pringle

Children in Changing Families: a Study of Adoption and Illegitimacy
Lydia Lambert and Jane Streather

A Fairer Future for Children

Towards better parental and professional care

Mia Kellmer Pringle
with

**F. S. W. Brimblecombe   Kay Carmichael
Ronald Davie   Jean Medawar   Colin Ward**

First published 1980 by
THE MACMILLAN PRESS LTD
London and Basingstoke
Associated companies in Delhi Dublin
Hong Kong Johannesburg Lagos Melbourne
New York Singapore and Tokyo

Printed in Great Britain by
J. W. ARROWSMITH LTD
Bristol, England

British Library Cataloguing in Publication Data

Pringle, Mia Kellmer
  A fairer future for children.
  1. Parenthood
  I. Title II. National Children's Bureau
  301.42'7   HO755.8

  ISBN 0–333–27669–8
  ISBN 0–333–27670–1 Pbk

Contents

vi   *Contents*

Contributors

Professor F. S. W. Brimblecombe, CBE
Consultant Paediatrician, Royal Devon and Exeter Hospital.

Ms Kay Carmichael
Senior Lecturer, Department of Social Administration and Social Work, University of Glasgow.

Professor Ronald Davie
Professor of Educational Psychology, University College, Cardiff.

Lady Medawar, MA, BSc
Director, Margaret Pyke Trust.

Dr Mia Kellmer Pringle, CBE
Director, National Children's Bureau.

Colin Ward
Education Officer, Town and Country Planning Association, and Editor of its bulletin, *Environmental Education*.

The views put forward are the personal opinions of the authors and not necessarily those of the National Children's Bureau.

1

Setting the Scene

Mia Kellmer Pringle

Before attempting to look forward and to predict likely – or at least desirable – changes in family life and the care of children, I want to consider some of the major factors in the recent past which may have led to current concerns and problems. Chief among them are the high incidence of stress, emotional disturbance and mental illness, both among the young and adults; the marked increase in divorce and hence one-parent families; and the serious rate of juvenile delinquency, crime and violence.

Might the 1939–45 war have had more pervasive and lasting emotional and social effects than has hitherto been realised? Since it was the first time that the whole civilian population, including children, were affected, this is perhaps a plausible assumption. The vast majority of those born in the decade between 1937 and 1947 grew up in a time of great anxiety, insecurity, change and danger; with fathers in the forces, many posted abroad, children were reared single-handed by mothers; moreover, as many mothers worked outside the home to help the war effort, their young children were placed in day nurseries; evacuation separated many children from their own homes; and then the return of fathers to their families and civilian life meant a further period of change and readjustment for all members of the family.

Those born during the decade in question are now between 32 to 42 years of age; by now most of them will be the parents of children aged between 10 to 20 years. May not the disturbed and disrupted childhood experiences of this wartime generation account – at least to some extent – for the increase in broken relationships in their own lives and for a higher proportion of couples who are unable to provide secure and loving care for their own children? These in turn are linked to mental health, crime and violence.

Of course, many other new factors have played a part, too – such as easier divorce laws, changing moral and religious values and more relaxed sexual standards. Bringing the world into the living room through television, including its commercialised portrayal of the affluent life and of daily violence, real as well as fictional, has had an obvious effect on social life and a less generally agreed influence on child and adult social behaviour. Also, the last 25 years have seen the rise of the welfare state, better educational opportunities for both sexes and greatly increased affluence for the vast majority; poverty has not been abolished but it is less harsh and crippling. Television and a fridge are now considered necessities, while obesity is a greater problem among children than malnourishment.

Indeed, during the 'swinging sixties' and early seventies, rising material standards and full employment led to a euphoria of constantly increasing expectations, summed up in the now curiously dated phrase 'you've never had it so good'. Why, then, the continuing symptoms of social disease and malaise, reflected in high rates of divorce, drug-taking, alcoholism, delinquency, crime and violence? Perhaps the experience of the last war holds yet another clue.

Because of the expected bombing of the civilian population, a great increase in the rate of mental breakdown was predicted; to deal with it, a large number of beds were set aside in hospitals. Though many cities suffered severe bombardment and many people lost their homes and their loved ones, the rate of mental breakdown and of suicide, as well as crime, remained low throughout the war years. Was this because a shared fate makes hardship and loss much easier to bear? And because it generates compassion, neighbourliness and a common determination to win through? Whereas greater affluence and conspicuous consumption create rising expectations, competitiveness, selfishness and envy?

If this analysis of past events has some validity, what are the lessons for the future? In what direction should we go to ensure a happier, more creative and more fulfilled future for today's children? In attempting to suggest some answers, I shall concentrate on four areas: the roles and expectations of men and women; patterns of parenting; early prevention and intervention; and the changing roles of, on the one hand, parents and, on the other, education, health and social work practitioners.

Other contributors will provide an historical perspective; discuss what alternative futures may be lying ahead for parents and children; consider how to promote good child health; how to improve school adjustment; and how to create more favourable physical environments for children.

2

The Changing Roles and Expectations of Men and Women

Mia Kellmer Pringle

The promotion of equal rights and opportunities for women has during recent years gained increasing support, reflected in new laws and regulations. Yet in practice relatively little has changed in the actual position or influence of women. This is similar to the fact that though women obtained the right to vote fifty years ago, their full emancipation did not make much headway during this period. Clearly, laws by themselves are not sufficient. Neither is it primarily a question of treating women as an underprivileged 'minority' for whom special measures are required; nor is the ideal of equality appropriate if this implies – as it does for some – that women must become more like men in their aspirations, values, behaviour and attitudes.

So far the principal gain has been the opportunity to participate – either for the first time or to a greater extent – in areas of life traditionally reserved for men. But surely this is not enough, and it does not touch the basic question. This is that equality does not necessarily mean 'sameness'. The central issue is how the roles and relationships of both sexes will have to change if women are to be enabled to take their place in society in their own way and in accordance with their own values.

The consequences of current misconceptions

Are there sex differences?

These misconceptions spring from the assertion that there are no inherent differences between the sexes and those that appear to exist are due solely to early 'sex typing', historical and traditional accidents and, above all, male chauvinism. And that having equal opportunities means having exactly the same opportunities: adopting the same life-style; the same attitudes, characteristics, tastes and interests; and even the same clothes and hair styles.

But surely no one would deny that there is a whole range of physical and physiological differences? Women's height, weight, strength, shape, general appearance and hormonal balance are evidently very different from men's. Therefore is it not also likely that there are temperamental differences? What is unjustifiable and misconceived is the belief that because women are different, therefore they are inferior.

Aping the male model

The fact that masculine characteristics are considered superior is surely a reflection of the distorted values of our immature, acquisitive and materialistic society? Why should being self-assertive, aggressive, competitive, status-seeking and thrusting be preferable to being caring, compassionate, tolerant, sensitive and reflective – generally thought to be feminine attributes? Indeed, they are quite essential for the survival of the human race; and it may well be that because only women can conceive and bear children, they have developed a greater capacity for nurturing and caring which has then been further enhanced by the traditional division of labour between the sexes.

The consequences of current misconceptions and stereotypes have had a number of unintended and harmful effects; ironically it is women themselves who have been most adversely affected. Three examples will serve as illustrations.

The first is that 'liberated' women tend to ape the less likeable characteristics of men. Thus they overvalue intellectual prowess, drive and ambition and become arrogantly aggressive, competitive and concerned with 'saving face'. Among the consequences are that smoking and its ill-effects have increased, compounded by the greater vulnerability of babies of smoking mothers; that heart disease is no longer a predominantly male affliction; and that the rate of crime among women is rising.

Another harmful effect of current misconceptions is that while women continue to be subjected to the twin social pressures of being expected to marry and then have children, at the same time they are made to feel they are 'wasting their education' or otherwise are remaining 'unfulfilled' if they choose to devote themselves full-time to their children's care. Indeed, many are brainwashed to seek as a desirable way of life the heavy burden of two jobs, paid employee and home-maker. (Of course I am excluding mothers who seek paid jobs because of economic necessity.)

A third consequence is that because caring for children has become so undervalued, many a mother is being deprived of the sense of achievement and recognition, as well as of joy, which ought to be her due for undertaking the most skilled, demanding and responsible job of all (Pringle, 1980).

Future directions

Motherhood by choice

These misconceptions are as prejudiced as the former assumptions had been that a woman could only be satisfied and fulfilled if she married and had children. In fact, women will in future have a much wider range of options both in their personal and their working lives. The availability of greatly improved contraceptive methods and more permissive sexual standards will give them both freedom and choice. It was the destiny of yesterday's woman to raise a family. Today it can be her choice. Tomorrow – I predict and hope – it will be only those with a strong and over-riding motivation and preference for home-making and child care who will undertake the raising of a family.

There is evidence that to some extent this may have already started to happen. Since 1964 there has been a decline in the fertility rate in England and Wales, which has become quite steep since 1970 (Bone, 1978). This seems to be due to three factors: a postponement of first births; a reduction in fourth and subsequent births; and an increase in childlessness by choice. That this decline is due to couples' decisions to have fewer children is perhaps most conclusively proved by the marked increased in elective sterilisation. While in 1970 only 6 per cent of couples interviewed had decided on this step, in 1975 the figure had risen to 14 per cent and on present trends a further increase is predicted.

The decline in the birth-rate appears to have halted recently and a slight upward trend has occurred but there is little sign that another baby boom is on the way. The fact that large families are becoming an increasing rarity is in line with trends in most developed countries (except where governments have given sizeable incentives to reverse this trend). It has been suggested that families with five or more children may fall as low as 3000 in Britain (Eversley, 1976).

The reduction in family size will by itself improve the quality of parental care. There are clear indications from research that children in large families are at a considerable disadvantage physically, educationally and in terms of social adjustment. This is not solely a question of low income – and hence a lower standard of living – since these effects of family size upon development operate irrespective of social class (Prosser, 1973). The greater the extent to which parental time, attention and maybe also patience, have to be shared, the less is available for each child; this seems to be as true in respect of psychological resources as it is of the family budget.

The postponement of the first child may also improve the quality of parental care since the couple will not only be more mature themselves but more likely to enjoy a better income and housing.

Thus motherhood by choice is in itself likely to improve its status. In addition, men, too, will have to make a deliberate choice of life-style when seeking a partner. The fact that for the first time in sixty years, there are now more males than females in the UK, will also make for quite profound changes in the attitudes of both sexes towards each other.

'Feminine' qualities in a new scale of values

Even more important is the gradual recognition that if we are to build a more just, civilised and mentally healthy society, then greater emphasis will have to be given to the supposedly 'feminine' qualities of compassion, consideration, conciliation and concern. For example, a number of the more enlightened international business concerns now require all their managerial staff to undertake 'sensitivity training'. It is precisely such sensitivity to human needs that mothers have developed over the centuries through rearing children and making a home. The handling and understanding of immature, illogical, necessarily self-centred and at times difficult young human beings require a high degree of managerial skills, tact, patience and applied psychology.

Today many young people (as well as some not quite so young) are disenchanted with contemporary society, a largely man-made world. Though it has much to be proud of in terms of scientific, technological and artistic achievements, it is in the sphere of relationships between individuals within societies as well as relations between different nations, that much progress remains to be made. This includes how to make the best, or the least detrimental, use of our new scientific and technological knowledge so that it serves the interests of humanity. The thrusting competitiveness and the resulting rat race, the assembly line production processes imposed by an industrialised society, the performance of routine tasks in huge white-collar bureaucracies have not led to a personally fulfilled life for the vast majority of men.

In seeking a more creative and happier mode of living, these so-called 'feminine' characteristics and values are beginning to be accorded a more prominent place, both in public and private life. The demand to restore a more human scale and to place greater emphasis on the quality of life, is gradually blurring, to some extent, the dividing line between the 'male' and 'female' worlds.

In turn, this may help to break down the unjustified and misconceived division between the traditionally separate worlds of home-making and employment. Rather than effecting a mere exchange or reversal of male and female roles, a new content will be given to being a fully participating member of society. This may then lead to a change of priorities of what constitutes a 'good life': the dogma of continuing economic growth and the desire to acquire ever increasing material possessions will be replaced by the recognition that fulfilment and contentment are more likely to come from satisfying personal relationships and from a stable, mutually supportive family life. From this children would stand to benefit most, both during the difficult process of growing up and then when they in turn become parents.

Marcuse said recently (1978): 'I don't care if it is considered sexist, but I welcome the non-violence, receptivity and tenderness of women. All domination up to date has been patriarchal. This could be the beginning of a new civilisation.' That such a shift and readjustment of values and attitudes will entail a quite fundamental rethinking of the patterns of relationships and co-operation between men and women goes without saying. But it is through this process that women are most likely to achieve equal rights and responsibilities.

Bibliography

Bone, M. (1978) *The Family Planning Services: Changes and Effects. A Survey Carried Out on Behalf of the Department of Health and Social Security* (London: HMSO).

Davie, R., Butler, N. and Goldstein, H. (1972) *From Birth To Seven* (London: Longman).

Eversley, D. (1976) 'Demographic change and the demand for housing' in M. Buxton and E. Craven (eds), *The Uncertain Future*, (London: Centre for Studies in Social Policy).

Maccoby, E. E. and Jacklin, C. N. (1975) *The Psychology of Sex Differences* (Oxford University Press).

Marcuse, H. (1978) 'Men of ideas', *Listener*, 8 February.

Pringle, M. K. (1980) *The Needs of Children*, 2nd edn (London: Hutchinson).

Prosser, H. (1973) 'Family size and children's development', *Health and Social Services Journal*, 4325 suppl., pp. 11–12.

3

Patterns of Parenting

Mia Kellmer Pringle

The current trend towards smaller families and deferred but com-
pressed fertility is likely to continue. At the same time, greater
tolerance towards different life-styles is developing. This should
include childlessness by choice on the part of those who place a
premium on personal independence, or on freedom from a permanent commitment to another person (whether the sexual partner
or a dependent child) or on a demanding, fulfilling career.

A good case could be made for two types of marriage. Where a
couple decide on a union without children, there would be little need
for a marriage ceremony, although many may still wish to have one.
Only a legal contract would be necessary to lay down the rights and
responsibilities of each partner, particularly in case they decide to
part. Such unions could be dissolved as easily as or even more readily
than is possible today.

The second type of marriage would be entered into only if both
partners wish to have children; given some necessary safeguards, it
could be postponed until a baby is actually on the way. This union's
salient feature would be a declared intention by both partners to stay
together at least until their children are aged 15 years or so, in order to
provide for them the security and the model of both a male and
female parent. It would be very difficult to obtain release through
divorce before the stated time and the couple would undertake to seek
marriage counselling in case of serious difficulties.

By making children's interests and needs paramount during the
period of their growing up, some curb may be put on 'casual'
parenting both by the imposing of legal constraints and the influence
of public opinion which would regard such action as irresponsible.
Childlessness by choice should come to be seen as a mature and

responsible decision, rather than as selfishness, which it all too often is labelled today. Instead, bringing into the world unwanted human beings should be considered as the most selfish and irresponsible behaviour – at present committed daily by scores of people with scant regard for the disastrous long-term consequences. So-called self-fulfilment is an immature and unrealistic motivation for having a child – there are many easier and far less damaging ways to this end.

Thus in future it would no longer be assumed that a married couple would necessarily wish to have a family. Raising children would be a deliberately chosen life-style, freely adopted by couples, who set great store upon lasting personal relationships and on the joys which children bring to those who really like them and who willingly undertake their care despite its demands in terms of financial and emotional commitment and sacrifice.

The consequences of current misconceptions

These misconceptions spring from a number of erroneous assumptions or misleading generalisations. Among them is the implication that a person is gainfully employed and working only if this is done for payment outside the home. Yet caring for young children and running a home involve much longer hours than most paid jobs; entail not only unsocial hours and overtime but also week-end duties and broken nights; and make demands not only on physical stamina and energy but also require intelligence, sensitivity, imagination and patience.

Another misrepresentation is to paint the world of paid work as being stimulating, challenging and creative while presenting home-making and child-rearing as a routine, boring, intellectually stultifying task.

In fact, it is probably the most creative and demanding work available to the vast majority of people; it is carried out in more congenial and healthy surroundings than the often hot, noisy, dirty, smelly and physically uncomfortable conditions prevailing in factories, hotels, restaurants, supermarkets, stores and other places of work; and is far removed from the tyranny of clocking in, conveyor belts, assembly lines and the repetitive monotony of mass production processes. Of course, a tiny minority of people, such as those in the professions, the arts and the media, enjoy the privilege of doing interesting and rewarding work, the pattern of which is largely at their own discretion. This in no way invalidates the general situation.

'Working' mothers

The claim that the vast majority of mothers now are or wish to be in full-time paid employment is another misleading generalisation. For one thing, there is nothing new about married women in the labour force (Laslett, 1972) and during this century their proportion has never dropped below 30 per cent and at present stands at about 38 per cent. True, the proportion of employed mothers with dependent children has increased from 27 per cent to 40 per cent between 1961 and 1971. Nevertheless, the majority of mothers with dependent children are not in paid employment. Moreover, the proportion who work full-time (thirty-five hours or more a week) is a small minority which has in fact decreased from 13.5 per cent in 1961 to 10 per cent in 1971. This means that of the total number of mothers working, only a quarter did so full-time in 1971 compared with half in 1961.

An even more significant fact is that the younger the children, the lower the proportion of mothers who work full-time. Only a tiny minority of those with under-fives do so (a mere 5.5 per cent, which rises to 18 per cent for those with children aged over 11 years). Indeed, a recent survey in inner city areas found that 75 per cent of women strongly believed that 'real fulfilment' lay not in a job but in a home and children (Marsh, 1979).

Yet it is being claimed by some that many more mothers would seek paid employment if satisfactory substitute day care were more readily available. Against this, it could be argued that many women, particularly with young children, who are in outside employment at present, would prefer to be full-time mothers if child-rearing and home-making were accorded the status their importance deserves; and if adequate financial support were available as of right for all who need it.

The denigration of child rearing

These misconceptions have had a number of harmful, even if unintended, consequences. Once again, it is largely women who have been most adversely affected. Three examples must suffice.

To begin with, the cumulative impact of the denigration and

undervaluing of child rearing and home-making have been very demoralising. So much so that women, who are fully stretched mentally and physically, respond to these confidence-sapping pressures by replying when asked what they do, 'nothing really'. Or, equally sadly, mothers confess 'you hear and read so often that looking after kids makes you feel trapped and resentful that if you enjoy it, you feel guilty or even that there must be something wrong with you'.

Yet raising the next generation is surely equal in importance to productivity outside the home? The economic argument that women's labour is required for the creation of wealth is as fallacious as that of denying women an equal access to higher education on the grounds that it will be 'wasted' if they become home-makers and mothers. Surely children are a country's most important 'raw material and future resource'; and research has shown that the mother's education is as closely related to a child's later achievement as is the father's (Davie *et al.*, 1972).

Next, it has been argued that caring for very young children is essentially boring and imposes social isolation which accounts for the high incidence of depression among mothers. Only by reading the small print, as it were, does it become evident that a high proportion of the women studied not only live in decaying urban areas and have unsatisfactory marriages but also that they had themselves experienced unsatisfactory mothering when young (Richman, 1978; Brown and Harris, 1978). The fact that in industry more working days are lost because of mental or psychosomatic illness, rather than physical complaints, is another indication that it is other environmental and emotional pressures rather than caring for children which account for the high consumption of tranquillisers and antidepressant drugs.

With regard to social isolation, it is surely not inevitable that solitary females should raise their children cooped up by themselves in flats or small houses? There is nothing necessarily 'middle class' about mothers sharing the care of children on an informal basis of friendship, as well as through mother and toddler clubs and preschool playgroups. In deprived areas or in new housing estates it has been shown that co-operative activities can be established not only in relation to caring for children but over a wide range of pursuits and interests (Leissner *et al.*, 1972 and 1977; Joseph and Parfit, 1972; Ferri with Niblett, 1977).

A third consequence is a demand for vastly increased day care facilities for the under-fives. Despite their high cost, especially if they are to be of good quality, this is being canvassed as the preferred solution rather than providing adequate financial support so that no mother of under-fives has to seek paid employment for financial reasons. Trade unionists seem opposed to maternity leave extended over several years on the grounds that it would seriously curtail the employment and promotion prospects for skilled or highly qualified women.

Surely these arguments are somewhat hypocritical? To begin with, the majority of mothers are neither skilled nor highly qualified, so they are unlikely to be penalised by leaving the labour market for a few years. Next, why assume that the adverse effects on career prospects are inevitable? On the contrary, but for the prejudiced attitudes of management and unions alike, child rearing could be looked upon as an occupational asset. Also if caring for children is not regarded as a responsible, demanding and skilled job, why then do we expect that enough women will be willing to offer adequate care to groups of other people's infants, either in their homes or in institutions?

The double bind of social pressures

Because of current misconceptions women in many developed countries are having the worst of all worlds. If they decide to have a career and not children, they have to withstand powerful family and community pressures. If they decide to become full-time mothers, then their contribution as home-maker with a young family is grossly undervalued. If they opt for combining a family with full-time employment then they lead an overburdened, harassed life. The mechanisation of many housework tools, frozen convenience foods and services such as laundrettes, have simply meant that mothers can get through a greater amount of work while the division of labour has not changed greatly among most families, where both parents are in full-time employment.

Instead women have shouldered additional burdens and responsibilities as well as paying the emotional price of feeling guilt about being unable to make wholly satisfactory substitute care arrangements for their children and regrets at not having sufficient time to enjoy and stimulate their development. Of course the burdens are eased considerably for those able to find part-time work. However, unemployment and new labour legislation are likely to make such jobs even more difficult to come by. There is also a privileged minority able to secure high-quality, reliable day care but for the majority these solutions are not available.

Future directions

There are some indications that these misconceptions are beginning to be challenged. Illich argues that

> modernised poverty . . . is the experience of frustrating affluence that occurs in persons mutilated by their reliance on the riches of industrial productivity. It deprives them of the freedom and power to act autonomously; to live creatively; it confines them to survival through being plugged into market relations . . . The opportunity to experience personal and social satisfaction outside the market is thus destroyed. (1978)

As I see it, home-making and child-rearing confer the freedom and power to act autonomously and provide the opportunity to experience personal and social satisfaction. Should they then not be classified as 'creative self-employment' rather than, as at present, non-productive or non-gainful employment?

Another indication is to be found in the fact that in the United States men are beginning to revolt against the practice in big multinational companies of 'career mobility', that is, the need to keep moving home for the sake of promotion. Increasing numbers are refusing to uproot themselves and their families, putting the need for a stable home life and roots in the community before career prospects. The demand for and gradual introduction of 'flexitime' – allowing employees to determine their own working hours, which may reduce commuting time since it makes it possible to travel outside rush hours – provides more time for family life and is a reflection of this same trend. Also the reluctance to work 'unsocial' hours may partly be symptomatic of this wish.

A rather different sign of changing views is the recent attempt to calculate in financial terms the worth of a wife and mother. Not only have judges awarded considerable damages for the loss of her 'services to the family'; but also the Liberty Life Assurance

Company valued a housewife's contribution by calculating how much it would cost her husband to pay outsiders for all the household chores and child care work if she died. This worked out at £114.80 a week (*The Times*, 14 March 1978). Significantly, only one husband in eighteen was reported to have taken out any form of insurance on his wife's life.

Politicians and various commissions have recently also turned their attention to the family. Thus Walter. Mondale, the Vice President of the United States, argued early in 1978: 'Our task must be to do more than lead a government that tolerates family life or pretends to be neutral about it. We must help shape a society which nourishes families and helps them grow strong and flourish. And there is no more important task.'

The Advisory Committee on Child Development of the US Department of Health, Education and Welfare outlined in a recent report (1976) the elements of an adequate system of child care services. This included a 'guaranteed minimum income system to ensure that all families have sufficient income for one or the only parent to choose not to work outside the home, without sacrifice to family or children . . . Parents should have the option, first and foremost, of raising their children at home, without sacrificing a reasonable standard of living.'

In the UK both major political parties at least pay lip service now to the central importance of the family with children. Cynics believe this to be partly a reflection of our party system and partly due to unemployment when mothers' return to the labour market is discouraged in order to keep down the unemployment figures. I believe it may well be a genuine admission that the needs of families, especially those with young children, have been disgracefully neglected in the past twenty-five years by both parties.

Possible patterns of parenting

There are, as I see it, at least six major styles of child-rearing, the strengths and weaknesses of which will be considered briefly in what follows.

1. One partner to undertake parenting on a full-time basis until the end of each child's compulsory schooling.

2. One partner to undertake parenting on a full-time basis until each child is at least five years old.
3. Truly shared parenting between the couple.
4. Both partners working part- or full-time, delegating part of their children's care to other people or to institutions.
5. Single-handed parenthood by choice.
6. Creating settings quite different from conventional family life, such as communes.

1. Full-time parenting

How many couples would wish to opt for one partner being a full-time parent until the children have left school? The answer is not known because no one has bothered to find out. At present more than half of the country's parents opt for this choice despite the financial hardships entailed and despite the psychological pressure from 'liberated' women. Many more couples might well choose full-time parenting if society were to place greater value on it and if financial support were available on an adequate scale.

To make an informed choice young couples need to know the advantages of full-time caring. It is unique in the sense that the mother (or the father for that matter) has the time, and the patience, to develop sensitivity to the baby. It enables her to recognise and adapt to his very individual needs. It is much more difficult for mothers who can give only hurried and preoccupied attention to become so closely involved in the child's earliest responses and learning.

No adequate substitute has been found (in Western society at any rate) for the one-to-one, loving, mutually enjoyable relationship, especially during the first few years of a child's life. This relationship is the essence of full-time, individual care. Such a two-way process promotes optimal progress. It fulfils the irreplaceable function of laying the basis for the individual's adjustment within society. The capacity for co-operation and social living has its roots in family life.

Of course this does not mean that the same person must provide uninterrupted care for twenty-four hours a day, single-handed. Quite the reverse. Even very young babies should become accustomed to being looked after by someone else for short periods. More fathers now actively share in the care of their infants and more might be willing to do so if their hours of work made this easier.

Most mothers welcome sharing care either informally with relatives and friends; or on a more organised basis with mother and toddler groups, pre-school playgroups, one o'clock clubs, and so on. Those who really like children, find caring for them interesting and rewarding. During the first five years more and faster changes take place than during any comparable period of time thereafter. Observing a child's progress and fostering it brings joy and creative satisfaction. The majority of women who feel this way must make their voices heard to counter the view that mothering is a dull menial chore. On the contrary it calls on all a woman's talents, skills and ingenuity.

For those who wish to be full-time parents two changes are required. First, to increase the status of parenting by recognising its unique contribution to the community. Second, to provide adequate financial rewards. Other countries, such as France, Hungary and Sweden have succeeded in both these aims – so why not try here?

2. Full-time parenting for under-fives

Early childhood experiences have long-lasting effects which are difficult to alter subsequently. Recent research shows how early 'early' is; the significance of even the first few weeks of life is now being documented. With time to enjoy the child and to encourage his progress, the mother accelerates it by her very interest and delight. If these facts were made more widely known, many mothers might choose to be full-time parents at least until their children are three years old or until they start full day school.

Of course, many a two- or three-year-old is ready to mix with other children for a few hours a week. Going to a playgroup, kindergarten or nursery school broadens his or her world. Also it makes the transition from home to school less abrupt, gradually weaning psychologically both mother and child. These experiences are a valuable complement to parental care. In turn, mothers themselves benefit if they can participate in community-based activities, such as pre-school playgroups.

Where couples choose this option of parenting, many mothers are likely to want part-time outside work once children go to school. Today this is a more difficult option than full-time work. To make it a practical proposition, two new measures are required. First, a wide range of refresher courses as well as training opportunities for those

their parents return from work. Otherwise they have to spend them unsupervised, either roaming the streets or alone at home, which exposes them unfairly to a whole range of undesirable and often dangerous risks. Such provision can justifiably be considered as an essential preventive measure in more than one sense. Exposure to such hazards as road accidents, drowning or fire risks would be reduced; opportunities for delinquency and vandalism would be curtailed; and having interesting and challenging activities available would stimulate children's intellectual and physical abilities.

5. Single-handed parenthood by choice

There has been much muddled and contentious argument about the merits of deliberately chosen single-handed parenthood. In particular, single motherhood is glamourised as a courageous, independent stance, proclaimed by ideological theorists but easily practised only by financially affluent women. What is the likely motivation for such a choice? Could it be a reluctance to share with and adapt to life with a partner? Such reluctance may be a contra-indication to the desire or ability to adapt and give priority to the needs of dependent and demanding children.

Sadly, this stance largely ignores psychological and even practical realities. For one thing, the child will lack the example or model of a male parent. For another, it will be deprived of the daily experiences of a man and a woman behaving lovingly and caringly towards each other. If parenting is an arduous and challenging task; if the child's long-term welfare should be paramount because of his helpless dependence; if sharing responsibility, both materially and emotion-ally, makes it less demanding; then surely single-handed parenthood has little to recommend it as a chosen style of child-rearing? Having to shoulder the whole burden of caring, of decision-making and of anxieties at times of stress – on what rational grounds can this be regarded as a desirable option? To go even further and encourage immature, unhappy, often disturbed teenage girls to keep their illegitimate babies seems to me irresponsible and against the best long-term interests of both mother and child.

None of this denies that one 'good' parent is likely to be better than two unsatisfactory ones or none at all; but these are not necessarily alternatives. There will inevitably always be some single-handed parents because of deaths, divorce and desertion, but single-handed parenthood should not be deliberately chosen. Research evidence shows, and commonsense supports, the fact that one-parent families, both adults and children, suffer in many ways. More adequate material and social support could alleviate some but not all of the ill-effects and disadvantages (Crellin *et al.*, 1971; Ferri, 1976).

6. *Alternative styles of group living*

For couples to choose a setting radically different from conventional family life is very uncommon. Communes have not been established long enough to assess their effects on children's development, but the largely anecdotal accounts which are available suggest once again that the interests of children are not well served. In any case, it is unlikely that this will ever become the choice of even a significant minority. For example, the findings from the Bureau's National Child Development Study indicate that the vast majority of today's sixteen-year-olds envisage family life very much along traditional patterns (Fogelman, 1976).

Some claim that the Israeli kibbutz has proved the viability of a communal social organisation. However, only a tiny minority (about 3 per cent) of the population live in a kibbutz. In any case, I very much doubt whether it is possible to transplant this system without the ideological and severely practical problems which led to its creation. Moreover, while child-rearing is shared from the earliest months of life between parents and professional educators, parental concern and involvement remain paramount.

The choice of the caring personnel as well as the pattern of care, are determined and supervised by the parents. Also children spend three or more hours daily as well as the week-end with their parents. During this time they are free from all the usual domestic and home-making responsibilities and able to devote their whole attention to playing with, talking to and enjoying their children. This is very different from the kind of half attention usually given for part or throughout the day in our society to pre-school children by mothers who are unavoidably busy with cleaning, shopping and cooking. Thus it is a very specific way of dividing the parental role which is unique in developed societies.

More recent evidence (personal communication) indicates that there is now a gradual return to more traditional family life in a growing minority of cases. In over 25 per cent of kibbutzim, the children not only sleep in their parents' home but also take at least one meal with them there; this continues until the age of seven – the start of compulsory schooling – and often later. This trend is on the increase as is the tendency for young kibbutz-reared women to prefer looking after their children and family themselves, rather than undertaking other work in the kibbutz.

The possibility of choice

In view of prevailing conditions and the needs of young children, only the first two patterns discussed – the two types of full-time care provided by one parent – will ensure their optimal emotional, social and intellectual care and stimulation. More choice will only become available if society's (and employers') attitudes were to change to accept the practice of shared parenting; and if a number of radical changes and modifications were made to substitute day-care facilities.

All types of pre-school provision would have to be available free of charge according to the child's needs and parental wishes. If for the time being the economic situation makes this impracticable, then would it not be fairer to provide free services for those in need and charge the others according to ability to pay? Equally important, all the advantages seem to lie in setting up integrated, multipurpose, pre-school centres on a neighbourhood basis, to provide both care and education. Such centres would offer much greater flexibility and thus be able to take account of changes in family circumstances, whether these are planned or unforeseen. The most suitable programme for any one child at any particular time would be worked out on the basis of careful initial observation and assessment. The appropriate balance between physical care, mothering, stimulation, adult-guided learning activities and child-initiated exploration could be determined and readjusted in the light of progress made; so could the frequency and length of time the child attends.

The degree and nature of the mother's (and father's) participation in the centre's activities could similarly be flexible but would always be actively encouraged. In this way, comprehensive pre-school centres would combine the best features of day nurseries, nursery schools and playgroups; they could also be available for use by child-minders.

In our materialistic society, where salary levels are important status symbols and where not to be 'unionised' means remaining at the bottom of the heap, the home-maker has now lost out even more than before. How much so is evident, for example, from the extremely small child benefits recently introduced (though they are at last paid also for the first-born child); and the fact that they have never been linked with increases in the cost of living. Thus they lag far behind increases in other benefits, such as old age pensions, which have been increased much more frequently to take account of inflation.

Adequate financial reward is required so that no mother of under-fives has to go out to work for financial reasons. Husbands should have to acknowledge the value of looking after young families by sharing their income with their wives as of right. Also the state should pay realistic responsibility allowances to the parent, whether married or single, who undertakes the child's full-time care.

In France and Hungary this is already done, the amount being related to the pay of trained teachers and being highest for infants under three years. In Sweden, either parent may take seven months leave on full pay after the birth of a child and about 6 per cent of fathers do so now. It is proposed soon to extend the period by a further five months. The longer-term aim is that children should be able to spend the first three years at home with one or other parent.

It has been argued that the view that very young children require full-time mothers is merely an ideological basis for the discouragement of day-care services. Might it not make more sense to turn this thesis on its head and ask: what are the ideological reasons prompting those who argue for vastly increased group care for the very young when countries such as Russia and Hungary, who introduced such care, are now reversing this very policy?

There would appear to be at least three reasons for this reversal in Russia. First, group care is now considered a very costly provision, especially if it is of high quality. Second, it is no longer regarded as being beneficial to children's emotional or intellectual development. For the under-threes, it is thought to be much better to be cared for by one and the same person, either their own mother or by what the Swedes call 'day mothers', a more accurately descriptive term than child-minders. Third, most mothers were found to prefer looking after their children themselves when given financial support so to do.

There is a need for wide-ranging and long-term cost-benefit studies in the UK of the respective advantages of paying really adequate allowances to mothers on the one hand, or, on the other hand, encouraging women to work full-time, while providing good quality child-care facilities. Also once children go to school, women who want to return to paid employment need to be provided with three facilities: child-rearing experience to be recognised as having enhanced – or at least not retarded – their career prospects; training opportunities or refresher courses; and shorter, more flexible working hours so that mothers (or fathers) can see their children off to school and be home when they return, as well as unpaid leave during their holiday periods and sickness.

Given the high cost of good quality group care, 'upgrading' both the status of and the financial support for parenting may well turn out to be the most cost-effective alternative in more senses than one. No longer would women feel obliged to apologise for being 'only a mother and housewife'. No longer would full-time mothers need to 'ask' for money to meet home-making costs. No longer would women be brainwashed into seeking the heavy burden of two jobs, worker and home-maker, as a desirable way of life. Devoting six to ten years – depending on the spacing of children – to their care would still leave her the opportunity for some thirty years of paid employment, whether part- or full-time.

If a couple decided to share parenting on a rotating basis, they would of course also benefit from the improved status and financial support, as would single-handed parents of either sex. In some families a complete reversal of parental roles may be decided upon for a variety of reasons and this too would be more acceptable in a changed climate of opinion that valued parenting more highly than is done now. In fact, couples would then be able to choose the style of parenting most suited to their needs. Also they would be able to change from one alternative to another as their circumstances and preferences changed.

Given such a transformed image and improved financial basis for parenting, it will be interesting to see which way couples will opt tomorrow.

Bibliography

Bronfenbrenner, U. (1977) *The Experimental Ecology of Human Development* (Cambridge, Mass.: Harvard University Press).

Brown, G. W. and Harris, T. (1978) *Social Origins of Depression: a Study of Psychiatric Disorder in Women* (London: Tavistock).

Cardozo, A. R. (1976) *Women at Home* (New York: Doubleday).

Central Policy Review Staff (1978) *Services for Young Children with Working Mothers* (London: HMSO).

Clutterbuck, D. (1979) 'Shorter working: more jobs or more problems?', *International Management*, July, pp. 23–6.

Crellin, E., Pringle, M. K. and West, P. (1971) *Born Illegitimate* (Slough: NFER).

Davie, R., Butler, N. and Goldstein, H. (1972) *From Birth to Seven* (London: Longman).

Ferri, E. (1976) *Growing Up in a One-Parent Family* (Slough: NFER).

Ferri, E. with Niblett, R. (1977) *Disadvantaged Families and Playgroups* (Slough: NFER).

Fogelman, K. (ed.) (1976) *Britain's Sixteen-Year-Olds* (London: National Children's Bureau).

Gronseth, E. (1978) 'Work sharing: a Norwegian example' in R. Rapoport and R. N. Rapoport (eds) *Working Couples* (London: Routledge and Kegan Paul).

Illich, I. (1978) *The Right to Useful Employment* (London: Marion Boyars).

Joseph, A. and Parfit, J. (1972) *Playgroups in an Area of Social Need* (Slough: NFER).

Kanter, R. M. (1976) *Work and Family in the United States* (New York: Russell Sage).

Laslett, P. (ed.) (1972) *Household and Family in Past Time* (Cambridge University Press).

Laslett, P. (1977) *Family Life and Illicit Love in Earlier Generations* (Cambridge University Press).

Leissner, A., Herdman, A. and Davies, E. (1972) *Advice, Guidance and Assistance* (London: Longman).

Leissner, A., Powley, T. and Evans, D. (1977) *Intermediate Treatment: A Community Based Action-Research Study* (London: National Children's Bureau).

Marsh, A. (1979) *Women and Shiftwork* (London: HMSO).

Pringle, M. K. and Naidoo, S. (1975) *Early Child Care in Britain* (London: Gordon and Breach).

Rapoport, R., Rapoport, R. N. and Strelitz, Z. (1977) *Fathers, Mothers and Others* (London: Routledge and Kegan Paul).

Richman, N. (1978) 'Depression in mothers of young children', *Journal of the Royal Society of Medicine*, vol. 71, no. 7, pp. 489–93.

Rossi, A. S. (1977) 'A biosocial perspective on parenting', *Daedalus*, vol. 106, no. 2, pp. 1–31.
The Times (14 March 1978).
Young, M. and Willmott, P. (1973) *The Symmetrical Family* (London: Routledge and Kegan Paul).

4

Why Prevention?

Mia Kellmer Pringle

A long-term comprehensive policy for children has so far been conspicuous by its absence. To be fully effective it would have to be based on improving the quality of parenting, of health care and of education from cradle to adulthood. Its achievement requires, in my view, three wide-ranging changes: first, a different attitude to parenthood and child-rearing; second, a willingness to provide more adequate supportive services for families and children; and third, the acceptance both of children's rights to consistent, continuing, dependable, loving care and of parents' obligations to provide it.

Intervention is likely to be more successful and less costly – in personnel, time and techniques – if it takes place not merely during the earliest years of life but during the earliest weeks and months; and most effective if a start is made with today's children – the parents of tomorrow. At present, we may well be paying the most for the least effective strategy, because prevention is not only better but cheaper than cure.

Granted more needs to be found out about how best to promote children's all-round development, surely enough is known already to take preventive action now? To use an analogy from the medical field: it proved possible to vaccinate and inoculate successfully against whooping cough and poliomyelitis without necessarily understanding why a particular child was more liable to contract the disease or how to cure it. Similarly, we have now an understanding of the broad preventive measures that would raise the general level of children's intellectual, educational, emotional and physical development. Hence instead of devoting resources mainly to vulnerable or disadvantaged groups, it is likely to be more effective in the long run –

both in human and financial terms – to apply these measures 'across the board'.

Aims of prevention

What should prevention aim at? There are three main objectives: to reduce the incidence of emotional neglect and rejection; to reduce the incidence of intellectual neglect and deprivation; and to reduce the incidence of handicap in childhood. To put it positively, the first aim should be to ensure that children acquire maximal emotional stability of life; second, to promote the development of all their intellectual and educational potentialities, so that they become fulfilled as individuals and effective as citizens; and third, to enable children to grow into physically fit adults.

The cost of prevention

How costly would it be to ensure that children's needs are met, so as to promote their optimal emotional, social, intellectual, educational and physical development? No one really knows because no serious consideration has been given to this question. How much would it cost to have supportive services available to the family, sufficient in quality and quantity, to prevent children who are 'vulnerable' or 'at risk' from growing up emotionally disturbed, socially deviant, intellectually stunted and educationally backward? Again, no one can say because the question has not been asked.

Some argue that as a society we simply cannot afford to pay either for wide-ranging preventive services or for comprehensive rehabilitation and treatment facilities. Is this not a fallacy? Surely the issue is whether we can afford not to do so? Failure to provide the necessary services and programmes for children and their families merely postpones the day when society has to pay a much higher price for not willing the means earlier. In the long run the cost is extremely high: not only in terms of human misery and wasted potentialities but also in terms of unemployability, mental ill health, crime and a renewed cycle of inadequate parenting. Even in the short run, it is by no means economic to do too little and to do it too late.

For example, emotional and learning difficulties in most cases begin to become apparent soon after a child starts school. Indeed, recent evidence shows that the best single predictor of educational failure at the age of sixteen years is the level of attainment reached by the age of only seven years. Hence if those children whose achievement is low at this early age could be selected for additional help, then later backwardness could to a large extent be prevented (Hutchison *et al.*, 1979). Providing small teaching units and school psychological or psychiatric services is inevitably costly. However, leaving matters until a child's difficulties are so severe or his family background so unsatisfactory as to lead to removal from home to a residential setting, the increase in cost will be tenfold.

Because there are at present not enough trained personnel in any of the helping professions – whether remedial teachers, social workers, psychologists, psychiatrists or speech therapists – waiting lists are long; only those whose needs are the most urgent have any hope of receiving special help early. The later it is given, the more difficult and lengthy, and hence the more costly, the treatment and the less hopeful the outcome. Thus in the event we are paying the most for the least effective intervention.

Another example of doing too little and too late relates to juvenile delinquency. There is now overwhelming evidence documenting the failure of most residential intervention strategies designed to curb it, whether they aim to re-educate, treat or punish the young offender. To bring about real and lasting changes in behaviour at this relatively late stage would require considerable resources to introduce properly planned, largely community-based schemes of rehabilitation.

Prevention is a rather blanket term and it helps to divide it into three stages or levels, namely primary, secondary and tertiary prevention.

Primary prevention

Primary prevention aims to bring about among all children a general rise in emotional resilience and to develop to the fullest their intellectual and physical potentialities. The driving force to translate this aim into reality must come chiefly from parents, aided by the skill and knowledge of paediatricians, psychologists and health visitors, all of whom are primarily concerned with normal development and with preventing handicap. Once the child starts school, teachers should take a major share in this responsibility.

Preparation for parenthood, including family planning, could make a vital contribution to primary prevention. Modern parenthood is too demanding and complex a task to be performed well merely because we all have once been children ourselves. One group whose needs are particularly urgent are those young people who have grown up deprived of adequate parental care. Having had no opportunity to observe and experience at first hand good parental skills, they will have little chance themselves of becoming in turn responsible parents.

An effective programme of preparation for parenthood should adopt a wide and comprehensive base. It must deal with the whole area of human relations and then more specifically with child development. First-hand experience of babies and young children should be an essential part of the programme; as should an understanding of the ways in which the relations between a married couple and their whole life-style are bound to change when they become parents.

Responsible parenthood must come to mean that the parental role has been freely and deliberately chosen in the full realisation of its demands, constraints, satisfactions and challenges. Since the technological know-how is now available it would be possible to translate into reality the slogan 'every child a wanted child'. Then there would be a much better chance than at present that the basic needs of children will be met.

Secondary prevention

The aims of secondary prevention should be threefold: to help families through periods of temporary strain and crisis; to improve and, where necessary, supplement the quality of care and education for children considered to be 'vulnerable' or 'at risk'; and to prevent the disintegration of the family unit when this is in the child's best interest. The keynote must be early and constructive intervention. Early because problems rarely spring into being fully fledged, nor does the maladjusted, backward or delinquent child do so; constructive in the sense that intervention should aim at enabling the child or family to cope again independently as soon as possible.

The broad categories of children 'at risk' are sufficiently well known to make early secondary prevention feasible. Briefly, there are five, not mutually exclusive, groups.

1. Socially and culturally underprivileged children, including some ethnic minorities.

2. Families where personal relationships are impaired or where there is emotional or physical neglect.
3. Families afflicted by serious physical or mental illness, or by a disabling handicap.
4. The child who has only one parent, be it because of illegitimacy, divorce or desertion.
5. Families stricken by severe and disrupting crises.

In all these circumstances parental care may become inadequate unless comprehensive support services are promptly made available.

Provision such as daily or resident home helps; educational visitors; day foster parents; nursery groups; classes and schools planned to meet the very special needs of the young underprivileged child; a 'prolonged' school day; adventure playgrounds, self-governing hobby clubs and constructive school holiday provision; parental counselling; family advice centres – these are just some of the possible measures to be taken.

In some cases secondary prevention may require long-term support. If this succeeds not only in keeping the family together but also in improving the quality of child care, then in the long run this would be an investment for the future. At present too many children from unsettled, disrupted and inadequate families grow up to become themselves the inadequate parents of another generation of emotionally and intellectually neglected children. Thus the vicious circle of unsatisfactory relationships, emotional maladjustment and educational backwardness is perpetuated.

Too often there is still a misplaced faith in the blood tie and an unjustified optimism about the chances of successfully awakening or rekindling parental interest when a child has been to all intents and purposes abandoned. In consequence thousands are condemned to remain in long-term public care without permanent substitute parents.

In a small proportion of cases, there is the danger that we so overvalue the child's ties with his natural parents that we are too slow to consider severing them permanently. This is so when the parents are severely and chronically disturbed themselves or totally rejecting the child. Thus some babies who have been brutally assaulted are returned to their homes when both common sense and clinical evidence indicate that there is a high chance of it happening again with the risk of permanent injury or death.

Tertiary prevention

The aims of tertiary prevention are twofold: to rehabilitate the emotionally maladjusted and the intellectually deprived; second, to counteract, or at least mitigate, the ill-effects which may result from children living for long periods, or permanently, apart from their own families.

The labels given to children whose behaviour deviates from what is acceptable tend to be based on a rather artificial classification. Whether a child is labelled maladjusted, requiring care and protection, delinquent, or needing to be taken into care, depends less on his or her own behaviour than on the agency by which and to which he or she is referred in the first instance. This is, in turn, determined by a combination of chance, local circumstances and social class.

For progress to be made, there is an urgent need to improve the quantity and variety of provision available for the assessment and the treatment of maladjusted, backward and delinquent children. This applies as much to the educational/social/psychological as to the medical/psychiatric approach. With any form of treatment (or their combination) full parental involvement is essential, whether the child stays in his own home or is removed from it. Otherwise he remains in, or returns to, the selfsame conditions which led initially to his deviant behaviour.

Children who have to live apart from their own families fall into three main groups:

1. Those needing frequent or prolonged hospital treatment.
2. Pupils attending boarding schools.
3. Children who have to be taken into care.

Each of these circumstances has different potential dangers for normal development, but they share one common feature, namely the danger of becoming 'institutionalised'. The younger the child, the more traumatic the separation from his family and the more potentially damaging its consequences are likely to be. Hence a major aim of tertiary prevention must be to make removal from home as constructive as possible. This means that it must become a more positive procedure than at present.

Positive child care

One way of achieving this is by setting up truly multidisciplinary assessment centres for all children who have special needs or problems. Their purpose would be fourfold: to provide a comprehensive medical check, which would include minor ailments, minimal neurological involvement and psychiatric conditions; to carry out a full psychological examination, which would cover emotional, social and intellectual development; to undertake a wide-ranging educational examination, which would include language development and scholastic attainments; and to assess the home background and family situation. In every case both strengths and weaknesses would be identified. Based on such an all-round assessment, appropriate plans to meet the child's needs could then be formulated and translated into practice, with progress being regularly monitored and reviewed.

The setting up of comprehensive assessment centres might lead to the abolition of our present rather meaningless labels. Then we may come to regard some children as 'in need of special care' just as we now consider some 'in need of special education'. The use of a similar nomenclature may serve to emphasise the fact that positive child care and constructive education have common aims: to make comprehensive provision for the fullest all-round development of children of all ages; to ensure early detection and intervention when difficulties arise; and to provide a wide variety of day and residential facilities to meet the whole range of individual needs. Approached in this way, early and multifaceted prevention may yet become a reality in our lifetime.

In what follows, the main emphasis and focus will be on primary prevention.

Bibliography

Davie, R., Butler, N. and Goldstein, H. (1972) *From Birth To Seven* (London: Longman).

Hutchison, D., Prosser, H. and Wedge, P. (1979) 'Prediction of educational failure', *Educational Studies*, vol. 1, no. 5, pp. 73–82.

Millham, S. L., Bullock, R. and Cherrett, P. (1975) *After Grace – Teeth* (London: Human Context Books).

Millham, S., Bullock, R. and Hosie, K. (1978) *Locking Up Children* (Farnborough: Saxon House).

Pilling, D. and Pringle, M. K. (1978) *Controversial Issues in Child Development* (London: Elek).

Pringle, M. K. (1971) *Deprivation and Education*, 2nd ed (London: Longman).

Pringle, M. K. (1980) *The Needs of Children*, 2nd edn (London: Hutchinson).

Rutter, M. and Madge, N. (1976) *Cycles of Disadvantage* (London: Heinemann).

Wall, W. D. (1975) *Constructive Education for Children* (London: Harrap).

Wall, W. D. (1977). *Constructive Education for Adolescents* (London: Harrap).

5

An Historical Perspective

Jean Medawar

This chapter endeavours to take a bird's eye or historical view of the sort of prevention we are all wishing to plan or promote. In general, I think it is damage – damage to the inherited equipment of a child, and, from birth onwards, from the environment to this equipment.

Planning prevention

Before any sort of damage to anything can be prevented, the nature of the damage and the nature of what is being damaged have to be understood. In the case of what can harm a child, there is so much to learn and so much still to be discovered that many different disciplines are concerned – genetics, embryology, physiology, biochemistry, psychology and history – most of them relatively young disciplines themselves. But long before these disciplines were born, poets and prophets and philosophers had had flashes of insight about the nature of man and about the influences that mould it. 'Man does not live by bread alone' is one of the best, and best known.

Gradually, the evidence that backs up the truth of the insights is being uncovered by the multidisciplinary research of this century. I have the impression that this research is being floodlit by two new concepts, each fully backed by evidence: one is the realisation that each individual is unique, and the other is a respect for the miraculous complexity and delicacy of the organisation of each new human being. These ideas contrast strongly with the old arrogance of certainty, founded more on ignorance than evidence.

The parable of the sower and the seed gave an early insight into the nature of man – created from the seed of his nature, and growing in the ground of his nature. Today we are beginning to understand the details of this story. Each individual is the unique result of interactions between what is inherited from the male and female germ cells of the parents and the physical, emotional, educational and social climates that form its environment. Little of this could be fully understood until Watson and Crick finally disentangled the beautiful helical puzzle of the hereditary material, and long-term studies of child development showed how easily a good inheritance could be damaged by a dull and loveless upbringing (Watson, 1968).

The whole business of preventing damage of any sort to the development of a child is a relatively recent idea – indeed the idea of prevention in general is new. Until roughly one hundred years ago, incurable disease, intolerable pain and infant deaths were largely unavoidable. Without an understanding of the causes, men were powerless to act. So we prayed for strength to accept whatever God or Fate had decreed for us – including the arrival and often sudden departure of babies and small children. Prevention was limited to intercessionary prayers, burnt offerings and nosegays for the judge.

Until Edwin Chadwick and Dr John Snow fathered sanitary engineering in the 1840s, before Pasteur discovered that many diseases were caused by micro-organisms and Lister began to teach antisepsis, most rules for preventing physical damage to the body were based on ignorance and legend. Cupping, purging, bleeding and beating for insanity added to the horrors of the illness.

Opposition to change

Prevention was hindered by the usual defensive reaction to any challenge to an old belief. Every new discovery in the field of health was at first regarded as an insult to piety, and a flouting of the Will of God.

When the first main sewer in London was to be laid in 1854, *The Times* complained that the British people would 'rather take their chance with cholera and the rest' than be 'forcibly cleared by Mr Chadwick and his friends'. But when the Prince Consort died of typhoid fever in 1861 the drains at Windsor Castle were examined and the cesspits were found contaminated and full to overflowing.

The use of anaesthetics was attacked as 'unnatural'; Simpson, who pioneered the use of chloroform, was called a 'decoy of Satan'. In my lifetime, a Pope assured a congress of obstetricians that the more pain a mother suffered during the birth of her child, the more she would love it. I do not believe that this travesty of the truth would be taught today.

In 1869, a Dr Beatty, in a letter to the *Lancet*, called birth control measures 'filthy contrivances' and assured the readers of the *Lancet* that the subject of contraception would 'never become a wing of the healing art'. He was not shown to be wrong until 1967.

Gradually, these new ways of preventing damage to health were accepted. They have been so widely accepted that it is hard for a teenager today to realise how recently they existed. It is easy for me because I can remember my grandfather and have read the diary he kept in 1864 when he was a young surgeon at Guy's hospital, and was in charge of the wine for the patients – not a pre-NHS luxury in the ward, but the only generally available anaesthetic.

New outlook for women

In the early part of the nineteenth century, the side-effects of the industrial revolution and the work of the sanitary engineers were reflected in the fall of infant deaths, and women's attitudes to children and to themselves began to change. Between 1801 and 1830, the population of England rose by $5\frac{1}{2}$ million – not because more babies were born, but because fewer died. As babies survived to grow and raise families of their own, women began to question the old pattern of pregnancy – as often as God willed – to replace the losses God had also willed. By the 1880s, the birth rate of 35 per 1000 began very slowly to fall, and by 1930 it was possible for five small pioneer birth control groups to join together to form what later became the Family Planning Association. From then on, one of the most influential forms of prevention grew steadily – the control of conception and the evolution of a choice of life for women was made possible by the combined effects of education and contraception.

In spite of opposition, the obstacles that had prevented most of the female half of society from pursuing careers other than motherhood were gradually overcome, until today it seems incredible that the Rev. J. W. Burgon could have thundered from an Oxford pulpit in 1884, 'Inferior to us God made you: and our inferiors to the end of time you will remain.' This was provoked by the proposal to educate young women '*with* young men and *like* young men'. To do so would, he said, 'defile their lovely spirit with the filth of old-world civilisation'. I think he meant the more robust passages from Juvenal.

Although opposition to both education and birth control were vitriolic, opposition to birth control as an idea, quite apart from the means used to achieve it, lasted much longer. Yet if ever a short history of women is written, the revolution produced by contraception in their lives may well be compared to that produced in men's lives by the invention of the wheel; but freedom to plan a family would have been a sterile victory if it had not been combined with the freedom to become educated and therefore free to create in other ways.

In the years between the two world wars, evidence accumulated that it was respectable to believe not only that one could, but that one should do something oneself to relieve God of total responsibility for one's life. For the first time in man's short history there was reliable information about the human constitution and the dangers to it from physical, emotional or social influences. Even if we did not yet know how to protect ourselves from bacteria, we knew that they and not a revengeful God made us ill. We had learnt something from Freud about the relation between mental and physical health, and how deeply childhood experiences might affect later development. People began to study what children needed and what sorts of conditions allowed the optimum development of whatever they had been born with.

Erik Erikson (1965) opened our eyes to the techniques planned and used by different societies to fit their children for the culture they were born into; and Carl Rogers (1961) showed that it was possible to extract an adolescent from the deepest and most anguished and inturned despair into an adult, capable of accepting and trying to manage his own and the world's affairs. Bowlby showed how early in life babies were conscious of the world around them and how much they learnt about it from the feel of those who were looking after them. Madame Montessori and Susan Isaacs at Margaret Pyke's Malting House School in Cambridge laid the foundations for modern playgroups and nursery schools. So the knowledge to give children a better chance than they had ever had before existed, even if the chances were not yet available to many.

During the Second World War, the knowledge of food values and vitamins was wisely used by the Minister of Food, Lord Woolton, and his adviser, Professor Jack Drummond, to prevent the harm that food shortages might have caused to the physical health of babies and children. Thanks to their planning, the wartime crop of under-fives, fed on essential foods and denied unnecessary ones, were the healthiest on record.

Evidence for the truth of the old insight that 'man does not live by bread alone' was clearly shown after the war by findings provided by a study of children in two orphanages in Germany. Each group had the same diet but each had a different house-mother. One group thrived much better than the other. Someone with curiosity and nerve caused an exchange of house-mothers, and soon the weights were reversed, demonstrating the nourishing value of TLC – tender, loving care.

Today

Now that so much is known about how to prevent damage to the marvellous endowments of a child, why are some 200 000 children born to parents who did not really want them? Why are so many mishandled that they become delinquent or violent? Why are 100 000 children in care? Why do so many parents look as if they did not much enjoy their children? Has planning failed? Of course, there is no single answer, and no universal remedy to prevent these mistakes.

One of the reasons for these miseries is that the Western world has changed more rapidly and more radically in the last two or three generations, than at any time in the short million years history of the human race. Even the 1930s are as foreign to the present generation as the Dark Ages. In the three generations, women emerged from the old stereotypes, men learnt to fly like birds – only at supersonic speed – to travel underwater like fish, to see and hear what is happening all over the world, to harness energy by splitting atoms and to reach the moon and study its structure.

Buy what you want to be

Understandably, the idea began to spread that man could not only help himself, but that he could do anything – he was really lord of all he surveyed. If science and technology could so greatly improve the world for men, then it did not seem so necessary for men to work at improving themselves. So the virtues they had aspired to and that had formerly stood them in good stead – patience, work, prudence, honesty and faith in these values – were overshadowed by new aspirations. Roughly: plans for improving oneself concentrated more on the supermarket than on do-it-yourself. Crudely, the idea was that you could buy what you wanted to be. I remember one advertisement that claimed to ensure friendship between a mother-in-law and a young bride. All she had to do was to sprinkle a certain white powder into her lavatory bowl. Expectations of abundance and affluence spread through society and made the morality of waste-not-want-not seem stingy or mean. So many machines could make life easier – and all you needed was money; if you had no ready money, you could buy them by instalments. The Old Testament had a phrase for it – 'whoring after false gods'.

By 1972, however, 112 of the nations in the world were beginning to realise the dangerous consequences of the new morality, and were alarmed enough to meet in Stockholm, under the auspices of the United Nations, to consult about the effect man was having on his environment.

The future

The summary of the consultations was shocking. By preventing early deaths from disease and failing to prevent unwanted births, the population of the world had reached three billion. If the current ratio of two births to one death continued, the three billion would double by the end of the century. Two-thirds of all these people go hungry to bed, two-fifths cannot read.

Demands for energy are trebling every ten years. Poisonous insecticides that had promised to preserve crops for man instead of for insect predators had worked their way, via rain water, into the rivers and down to the sea; there they passed into the bodies of plankton, via them to shrimps and on into fish, to appear finally in the fat of Antarctic penguins. The lessons to be learnt from Barbara Ward's book *Only One Earth* (1972), written for the Stockholm conference, were now up on the world's blackboard for all who could read to see.

The evidence for the truth of the insight which declared that 'we are all members one of another' was now documented. Man, the smartest and most numerous of all the earth's large animals, had forgotten it. He had learnt to break the old cruel cycles of life and death, of use and re-use of materials, and had become tipsy with power. We, the humans in the West, had become so smart we were cutting ourselves. In particular, we were cutting ourselves off from an understanding of and respect for the earth we had grown up on. The supermarket view of the future had led to a precipice. All this change was enough to flutter the stoutest heart and bewilder the brightest. Parents had a hard time when the old authorities and landmarks were no longer credible or visible; failure to build a strong framework of goals and limits did not do much for children.

The events of 1973, the year after the Stockholm conference, delivered another shock. The price of oil rose out of reach for many, and geologists warned that the supply was not inexhaustible – it would start dwindling in the 1990s. So many hopes and plans had been built on oil, and on hopes of affluence, that the shock was seismic. Retrenchment is rarely an attractive policy.

In the second place, it looked as though our plans to save our children from dying of smallpox, malaria, typhoid and sleeping sickness merely commuted a former death sentence into a life sentence: millions in the East were starving, uneducated, helpless and despairing, and the numbers were daily increasing. No wonder so many have come to feel that the best plans we can make against calamities are themselves disastrous.

Hopes for the future

I would like to finish by giving my reasons for believing that our present enormous problems may not be insoluble. What we are living through may be one of our darkest hours – but we have not lost the capacity to change our ways. We have made terrible mistakes, but that is natural for a species as young and inexperienced as the human race. We are young and may therefore hope to improve.

We have been given the unique gift of self-consciousness – of all living creatures, we alone can look back into the past, a little way into the future and, by a tremendous contortion, back at ourselves and at our mistakes. Recognition of a mistake is the first step towards not making it again. We are the most unspecialised creature, able to adapt to many different circumstances. Rats, for example, get desperate when they are overcrowded – and so do we. But we have the ability to plan our way out of the difficulty – if we choose.

The visible consequences of continuing to over-reproduce and overconsume are not hard for the next generation to grasp. When the facts are given they understand very quickly that too many people, taking too much from one finite earth, is a recipe for extinction. I know from the experience of running an educational experiment called 'Lifeclass', with a group of friends at the Margaret Pyke Centre, that even underprivileged 16-year-old boys and girls from Inner London schools are hungry for some sort of help in finding out who they are, what they can do, what choices they have. They want and need to know how much creative power they have. The most obvious is the power to reproduce and their ability to choose how they use it. The next generation has the chance to help build a society in which bearing and rearing children would be understood as a special form of privilege for which not every man and woman is suited. People whose talents for creation can be expressed in different ways should be equally respected and valued.

Above all, everyone needs to realise how much their individual choice matters, whether the choice is to reproduce or not, to overconsume or not. Whatever our talents, at least most of us can become involved, in however small a way, in planning to prevent everything that restricts or harms the development of each new infant's marvellous endowment of equipment for living.

Bibliography

Aries, P. (1962) *Centuries of Childhood* (London: Cape).

Bowlby, John (1952) 'Maternal Care and Mental Health: a report prepared on behalf of the World Health Organisation as a contribution to the United Nations Programme for the welfare of homeless children' (Geneva: WHO).

Bowlby, John (1969) 'Attachment and loss.' *Attachment*, vol. 1; *Separation – Anxiety and Anger*, vol. 2 (1973) (London: Hogarth Press).

Erikson, E. (1965) *Childhood and Society*, rev. edn (London: Hogarth Press).

Isaacs, S. (1932) *The Nursery Years*, rev. edn (London: Routledge and Kegan Paul).

Magee, B. (1965) *Towards 2000: The World We Make* (London: Macdonald and Co).

Medawar, P. B. (1972) *The Hope of Progress* (London: Methuen).

Morris, J. (ed.) (1978) *The Oxford Book of Oxford* (Oxford University Press).

Rogers, C. (1961) *On Becoming a Person* (London: Constable).

Simpson, G. G. (1969) *Biology and Man* (New York: Harcourt Brace).

Smith, J. M. (1972) *On Evolution* (Edinburgh University Press).

Vallery-Redot, R. (1902) *Life of Pasteur*, trans. R. L. Devonshire (London: Archibald Constable).

Ward, B. and Dubos, R. (1972) *Only One Earth* (Harmondsworth: Penguin).

Watson, J. D. (1968) *The Double Helix* (London: Weidenfeld and Nicolson).

6

Alternative Futures for Parents and Children

Kay Carmichael

My aim is to question myself and other middle-class, academic and professional people about our attitudes to poverty and the poor. It is time to examine the assumptions on which our behaviour and practice are based. All of us share feelings of helplessness in the face of the problems involved in enabling the poor to escape from their poverty. Practitioners and academics are increasingly uncertain about what can be done to make such escape possible. I want to discuss reasons for that uncertainty and some alternative styles that may be emerging. Increases in unemployment as a result of technological change could mean that much larger numbers than we ever envisaged could be transferred into poverty. Our concepts about who are the poor may have to change.

We may also have to examine the values of this advantaged society into which we are trying to pull disadvantaged people. Is it really so marvellous? Are our attitudes and ways of life so desirable? There is the possibility that the poor may have a contribution to make which will help us, the rich, to adjust to a future which will have more leisure than as yet some of us know how to cope with.

What does seem certain is that we cannot allow inequalities to grow between those of us who are poor and those who by contrast are rich. Not only does that offend against our long-held principles of social justice, it is politically not tolerable; even if it were, we should not want it. We have to create, deliberately, for the survival of democracy, a more just, equal, interdependent and creative society.

Who are 'the poor'?

When we use the phrase 'the poor' we find ourselves caught in a web of qualifications, ambivalent attitudes and embarrassment. We do not enjoy the candour of the Victorians in talking about the poor nor their satisfaction in being able, by contrast, to define their own prosperity. Even to concede the existence of significant numbers of poor people in our society has been a bitter experience for those of us who remember and participated in the reconstruction period of the post-war years. For younger people brought up in a welfare state the confusion is compounded by the lack of the obvious stigmata of poverty which had been defined in the 1930s in terms of slum housing with no sanitation and children going to school without shoes.

There is no difficulty in recognising the poor of the Third World. UNICEF posters show us the swollen bellies of children suffering from malnutrition; television shows us adults queuing for a bowl of rice, sleeping and sometimes dying on the streets of Bombay. That is clear and understandable, arouses our distress and sometimes the urge to help. These are poor people who have no opportunity to be anything else, they have no welfare state to help them, being poor is not their fault.

The homeless and rootless

In our own country the problem becomes more complicated. Who, here, are the poor? Some we can identify quite easily. As we walk through our major cities we will, if we choose to look, see some men and an occasional woman dressed in ragged dirty clothes, sometimes begging rather unobtrusively, sometimes sitting on a bench or pavement. They may be drinking or in a stupor. Some can be seen raking through the litter bins in the centre of the town fishing out bits of discarded food and eating it. They seem mostly older men but you can be startled and obscurely disturbed to see a quite young fellow behaving in this way. It is also more disturbing to see unkempt and disordered women clearly poor, unsettled and rootless than to see men in this state. To see children would nowadays be intolerable.

Emotionally we deal with these experiences by rationalisation. Of course no society is perfect, these people are probably mentally ill and simply unable or unwilling to use the services we have provided for them. It is a mark of an open society that we publicly tolerate such deviants. They are the dregs and we have to live with them but we expect them to keep a low profile. The police have instructions to move them on from the public benches or station waiting rooms so that the rest of us are not too embarrassed by them. The DHSS provides reception centres and voluntary organisations, night shelters. We sanitise the problem.

The poor who live in houses

Less definable is the great army of the poor who live in a more formal structure. They may be in a state of temporary, compulsory separation, in a prison, children's home or approved school, but what they do have – as distinct from the vagrants – is a base amongst a human group, no matter how small, of family or friends who live in houses. Some of the younger people may in times of crisis move from house to house, they may even on the odd occasion 'sleep rough' but they think of themselves as people who live in houses.

It is necessary first to make clear a distinction between those who are seen as the 'respectable' poor and those who are regarded as the 'non-respectable'. This distinction derives directly from Poor Law separation of 'deserving' and 'non-deserving' poor which still pervades our thinking. It is rooted in the work ethic: those who work and pay their own bills and are clean even though they are poor, are respectable. Those who do not work are not normally respectable unless they are old, sick or disabled, or looking after young children single-handed. If you do not work, are not sick or disabled and appear to have accepted that state as permanent, you deserve no respect. These attitudes seem to be held by the majority of the public and are reflected in the behaviour and responses of, among others, many local and some national politicians, officials of various departments, some landlords, shopkeepers and sections of the media.

The working poor

As a community we decided to establish as a right a basic level of income defined by Parliament, below which no one is allowed to fall. This applies both to families in work and to anyone out of work. Those families with children in full-time work, who are paid below the level Parliament considers appropriate are subsidised by a Family Income Supplement to bring them up to that level. This is the group we now call the 'working poor', but they are not thought of as 'the poor' by others nor normally by themselves. Yet they are poor if by poverty we mean lack of necessities using Adam Smith's definition:

By necessities I understand not only the commodities which are indispensibly necessary for the support of life, but whatever the custom of the country renders it indecent for creditable people, even in the lowest order, to be without. (Smith, 1776)

This group is often resentful of their dependence on welfare benefits and is aware of the indignity of means testing although it enables them to have among other things free school meals, prescriptions and rent and rate rebates. They are often semi-skilled workers, some are public service workers who are unionised and seek through their unions a way out of their poverty. They do not normally question the right of more skilled workers to have a higher standard of living – a motor car, holidays abroad – but they want to see themselves and their children participating as full members of their local community. They expect to be able to send their children away on school trips, to give wedding presents to members of their families or friends who are getting married, to pay their bills without too much difficulty. Budgeting skills are important to them. They may often feel helpless but never totally powerless. They will feel entitled to approach their shop steward or their local councillor. They might even consider joining a political party.

Their strength comes from their regular participation in the labour market. This gives shape and purpose to their lives and to the lives of their families. They will be wakened in the morning, probably by an alarm clock, in itself an important symbol of regularity, and the whole family will be roused including the children. If the parent takes a 'piece' or sandwiches to work, this will have required planning the previous day to make sure that there is bread in the house and something to put between the slices. Money will have been planned over the week to make sure there is something for every day and also for daily fares. The expectation of someone leaving the house regularly each morning can be shared by the children who will get ready for school. The parent's concern about his or her appearance in the eyes of workmates, particularly if in a clerical job, will be reflected in the entire family's care for its appearance so that the children going to school will be learning the importance of the presentation of self.

In a two-parent family when the children are old enough the mother may often take a job, if there is one available, even though this is included in the income assessment and may take the family out of the range of benefits. She too will have a sense of being a participant in the labour market and will organise the household around the needs of work. This in turn will make the children's relationship with school easier and more relevant since working parents are more likely to go to bed early. These groups are less likely to live in the most disadvantaged areas of council estates since regularity of work pattern can be a factor in housing allocation policies. Public perception will not necessarily be of the family as 'poor' but if so they will also be seen as respectable.

The sick and disabled

The very dependent poor, the sick and the disabled, some single-parent families, are categories of the dependent poor, who may have children and who are prevented from participating in the labour market. Medically certified sickness (or disability) is in one way the easiest situation for families to cope with. Each of us needs to define our lives in terms which make sense to us not only at a private but also at a public level. For an adult to be able to say that he or she has to be dependent because of a socially acceptable sickness or disability gives that dependency some dignity. There is some evidence that during the depression of the 1930s, the development of a psychosomatic illness was a way of enabling some unemployed to maintain their self-esteem.

Even within the sicknesses or disabilities there exists a hierarchy of status. Pneumoconiosis wins more respect than a bad back; a war or industrial injury more than having been knocked down by a bus when drunk. This hierarchy is reflected in the resultant income but more in the way people feel about themselves and inevitably in the way the whole family sees itself. Mental illness and mental handicap both bring quite specific problems of low status but also of uncertainty and irregularity of behaviour within the family which can accentuate a public definition which brings together concepts of the family as being both 'poor' and 'non-respectable'. They are frequently also marginal members of the next group.

The unemployed

The unemployed fall into two main categories, those who are in and out of work with some degree of regularity and those who have come to accept unemployment as a way of life. The former group is very much at the mercy of the market forces. In times of high levels of employment, they will all be mopped up, in recession they will all be unemployed. If the recession, as is happening at the moment, goes on for any length of time they will slip imperceptibly into the second group, and thereby have the lowest level of income of all groups on social security benefits. Their poverty is compounded by their non-respectability.

The life of poor parents with children

When they can work they are in the least skilled of the industrial jobs. They cluster in our cities and to survive, either in or out of work, have to be able to cope with a highly advanced and sometimes unsympathetic bureaucracy of social security, health, employment, housing and education services. They are the people who live in the houses for which there is least demand, either in the inner city or in the least popular of the bleaker housing estates and they will have less security of tenure. They will have less access to a motor car than other people and if living on a council estate, the poorest transport services. They will be less likely to have a telephone or to have friends who have telephones. They will be less likely to read newspapers, have books in their houses, have a bank account, a washing machine, a refrigerator. They will be less likely to go on holiday or to buy new clothes for themselves or their children. They are more likely to go to jumble sales than other people, to buy a tenth-hand chair or an old piece of linoleum and have the children carry it home. They are more likely to live in broken down or vandalised buildings, be more exposed to violence both within the family and on the streets. They will be less protected from exposure to deviant behaviour of all kinds. Their children will have more opportunity to be delinquent, to truant, and are more likely to be taken into care. They are much less likely to succeed educationally.

In coping with the constant shortage of money, the mother is less likely to find gratification in her role as home-maker than other women since she has fewer resources with which to create a comfortable home or make good meals and there is constant discrepancy between her expectations and her resources. The mother is also more likely to be anaemic and to be either depressed or anxious.

The low self-evaluation common among this group of the poor

means that they are less likely to value and cherish their bodies. They tend by reflection back from the world to think that they do not matter as people and this is generalised. A body which does not function properly becomes just another aspect of life which does not work for them. Low body esteem can apply by extension to children and there can be a resultant indifference to minor illnesses. This is reinforced by the poor quality of services normally available in the poor areas of the cities. Slum practices in health and dentistry do not encourage preventative medicine – perhaps realistically – since the general practitioners and dentists must wilt in the face of the poverty they confront every day.

The multiply deprived and self perception

This is the group we have learned to call the multiply deprived – deprived in income, housing, education and health. Every social group acquires complex sets of conceptions that express their sense of what their own lives and the life around them is all about. There are two main perspectives: what life ought to be; and what life really is. For the multiply deprived the accumulating experience of growing up – schools, jobs, housing – progressively destroys their belief in the 'good' life.

The powerful people in our society project the image of what life ought to be. For each of us there are different powerful figures which can vary in their significance in our lives. They may be religious, political, intellectual, sporting, artistic, industrial. At times the values they represent may be contradictory: we may want to make money but follow Christ in poverty. But generally our society has value norms to which most of us subscribe. Desirable values tend to be youth, beauty, wealth, ownership of consumer goods and status which has normally been acquired through work and earnings. These are assumed to add up to happiness and are presented with vicious regularity on our television screens. For example, when you buy a new breakfast cereal for thirty pence you are also buying the dream of the modern kitchen, the good-looking husband, his job, the loving wife, the laughing children.

For this assumption to be effective there has to be some degree of congruence between the dream and the reality. Some mornings have to be like that, or at least sufficiently like that to keep the dream alive. For the multiply deprived the lack of congruence is too great. Those who live below the conventional norm sense their own exclusion and accept it. They are not isolated as they used to be from knowing about it. Very few will not have a television set; for the unemployed it has become a real necessity.

Because of the improved expectations of the average worker, the unemployed will meet people, in shops and pubs, who have been in an aeroplane, gone on holiday or to an international football match. They will know constantly that this is outside their own range of choice. When only the rich travelled, had motor cars, ate in restaurants, this direct awareness of lack of opportunity for themselves and their children did not arise to the same extent. The multiply deprived poor are keenly aware that they are rejected by and are apart from the wider community and they learn this lesson early in life. Most of all they learn that they have no power to change that situation. They have no leverage, they cannot go on strike, their labour power is worth nothing; they cannot boycott shops, their spending power is too low to matter; there is no point making a nuisance of themselves, the police could arrest them with immunity; they have nothing to bargain with.

How did they get that way?
The poor have little history if one detaches them from the working class. They wrote no speeches or letters for posterity, carried no banners, had no leaders to give them visibility. They are recorded sometimes in local authority minutes describing measures to be taken against them or to control them. Sometimes artists have been caught by the drama of their misery and painted or drawn them. They have been studied by sociologists and psychologists. The economics of poverty have been examined as has the relationship between poverty and housing opportunity, poverty and health opportunity, poverty and educational opportunity. We seem to have institutionalised their existence, given them a permanent role assuming their continuance: we assume also that they were always with us and to an extent this is true, but only to an extent.

The pre-industrial society had recognised three groups of social casualties, the dependant (the old and the young), the handicapped (born that way), the disabled (temporarily or permanently through illness or accident). These were, in the main coped with by the auto-regulative kinship system. The industrial society had created a fourth class, the unadaptable, and the value system was unable to cope with this emergent group. The protestant ethic had focused on the idea that work, in the sense of paid employment, resulting in prosperity was proof that the worker was a good person. Inward spiritual goodness became symbolised in outward material success and not to prosper became a sign of wickedness. The poor symbolised the sinful and to remain poor was to be seen as unrepentant. Techniques for shaming the poor were sanctioned in charity and state intervention in welfare and inevitably the poor internalised these values and felt ashamed of themselves.

The cultural values developed around the work ethic were inextricably linked to developing a human being who would make a good, loyal, ambitious worker. To be successful the young had to be trained to be competitive and achieving, independent, to have high levels of self-control which included postponing gratification and therefore encouraged the thrift necessary to accumulate savings for capital investment in new industries, and to develop the capacity to endure distress stoically. These values informed the lives of the majority of people in this country until comparatively recently. That majority had developed in the main from those who had come by choice from the land into the expanding industrial towns.

There was another group, immigrants, who came, not by choice, but driven off their land by hunger. They came reluctantly, bringing with them to cities like Glasgow and Liverpool a Pandora's box of bitterness and resentment. Many carried with them, and have retained through the generations since, a pre-industrial culture of anarchic and transcendent life-styles characterised by interdependence, spontaneity and a great capacity for joy. Many found it difficult to abandon the inner rhythms of their lives for the factory whistle and the monotonous regularity of the machine. A Glasgow Sheriff said, 'getting a Highlander into the factory is like putting a deer to the plough'.

Many of the Irish found navvying jobs not only easier to get because the indigenous population did not want such low grade work, but more acceptable to their spirit of autonomy and the recollection of open air life. Some failed totally to be absorbed into the expanding economy, failed to identify with the work ethic and retaining their own values have continued from one generation to the next to live on the fringes of the economy, always as marginal people – our permanently rejected undeserving poor. When the economy booms, they are swept in to jobs no one else wants to do, when the economy recedes, they are the first to be laid off. They have been essential as a floating labour force, maintained at subsistence level when they are not needed, and expected to train their children to take over from them when they are old enough.

True they present certain problems. Because they are marginal to the economy, they have no great identification with it or loyalty to it. This is interpreted by their employers as a lack of responsibility.

They are the equivalent of the conscripted cannon fodder who were not expected to have any understanding of the technology or philosophy of the war they were fighting. For this reason the educational system set up to provide literacy for skilled factory workers had little relevance to them. Many, particularly those from Ireland and the Highlands of Scotland, had enough to cope with learning a new language without learning to read and write as well: they settled for labouring and non-literate work. Unlike the peasants who had come from areas where literacy was a norm they brought only an oral tradition. It was often a rich tradition of song and story, now identified as a valuable folk culture but at the time seen as lower class and vulgar.

Their relationship with authority must always have been ambiguous. If they had left the land unwillingly and in poverty there would be little enthusiasm for the problems they would have to encounter in the town or for the employers and landlords with whom they would have to cope. Many would bring with them a history of hatred of landlords and government. The zealous social control measures implemented by the sanitary inspectors in midnight visits to clear overcrowded houses, for example, cannot have endeared the new authorities to them. Nor would the behaviour of the Poor Law officers convince them that their poverty was their own fault. Some of the poor still, miraculously, reject that view.

What they did learn was that the world is a difficult place in which to survive and they passed that view on to their children along with some basic techniques for survival, many of which are unacceptable to the wider society. Attempts to restrain the behaviour of the poor or to change it, have widened from the deterrent or retributory styles of the Industrial Revolution to rehability models and now hover uneasily between them. The police and the courts represent one end of the spectrum, social workers the other. The poor learned that their behaviour was unacceptable and that it would always be under scrutiny. Up until now they have in fact been very easily contained;

their antisocial behaviour has been relatively inexpensive. It would cost much more to give them economic equality. Perhaps that is why as a society we seem reluctant to make any commitment to eliminate poverty.

The history of intervention

We continually attempt small programmes of intervention into the lives of families living in communities of poverty and we have an elaborate social security system which attempts to mitigate its effects. However, no one seems to think that we could have a society without the poor as a permanent class. We assume they will be there to clean our houses and offices, peel vegetables in our hospitals and sweep our streets; we assume that treating them or studying them will provide us with jobs as social workers, health visitors, administrators or academics.

We settle for trying to rescue individuals in the family from continuing in poverty by changing their behaviour in ways that will make them more acceptable to employers and bureaucracies or, in the case of children, to their school teachers.

The emphasis is squarely on the individual adult or child to adjust to and acquire the values of the wider society, to become ambitious, independent and more self-controlling in postponing immediate gratification. Small attempts are made to engage employers, bureaucracies and school teachers in 'understanding' and 'helping' the poor to join the rest of us but the final arbiter is always the demands of the economy and the state of the market. Those who cannot, or who choose not, to compete in work or in school are labelled uncooperative or inadequate.

Practitioners and academics are increasingly uncertain about the effects of intervention. It was not always so. In the 1960s we experienced in this country a period of intense, expansionist belief that the economy would go on producing more and more goods and that the standard of living for everyone would rise on an ever-developing curve. The poor, who had recently been rediscovered to exist in significant numbers, would share in this expansion. This optimism generated the energy to set up among others, the great inquiries into education and social work. Both Plowden (1967) and Seebohm (1968) saw poverty as a significant component of the systems they were examining. Plowden was the bolder of the two in tackling the question directly by recommending the setting up of educational priority areas as a way of intervening in the lives of poor children in primary schools (Central Advisory Council, 1967).

Forms of intervention

In July 1969 the first Community Development Project was announced. It was to be 'a neighbourhood based experiment . . . finding new ways of meeting the needs of people living in areas of high social deprivation'. The following year, twelve project teams were set up round the United Kingdom. They appeared to share the assumption that the cause of poverty lay essentially within the individuals' lack of certain agreed capacities and that these could be stimulated or activated by information services, leadership and conventional opportunities for self-actualisation.

They might well have made a more significant impact in a booming economy with jobs available for everyone but we will never know how valid their assumption was; the resources made available were much too inadequate to make an impression on areas which were in any case slipping further into the decline of employment which in the early 1970s was beginning to affect the whole country. Project workers began increasingly to state publicly their perception of poverty as a direct consequence of inequalities in the political and economic system. One by one the projects closed down. Optimism diminished and credibility was strained.

With primary school children attempts have been made at intervention varying from the educational priority areas based on the twin notions of positive discrimination and action research, to small imaginative projects around the country which often included the pre-school child.

Discussing the apparent failure of short-term intervention projects, (DES, 1974a) Halsey pointed out that one response to the apparent failure of these projects had been pressure from the professionals for more total programmes 'for the child to join almost at birth, and ideally to be in some form of residential care'. This is of course a classic response of professional groups to failure. It avoids questioning basic assumptions about the nature of the problem with which they are dealing.

Another response he described was 'to try to change the dynamic forces in the child's experience – to "multiply" the effects of the programme'. This latter approach has led to an emphasis on the home visiting strategy which stresses the interaction between the mother and the pre-school child as a crucial factor in the child's educational equation. The notion that with support from professionals the mother can become a partner in the process is attractive to some educationalists as long as the basic assumption continues to be that it is the reality of the school which is over-riding and the value sets of the teachers or project workers which have validity.

Wilson and Herbert (1978) force one to question that assumption. They compared a sample of severely socially handicapped boys with their less handicapped class mates, examining in detail how the varying degrees of deprivation influenced ability, attainment and behaviour; they concluded that:

Compensatory measures in the nursery and at school do not alter the long-term educational prospects of disadvantaged children. Our views are strengthened by the findings of Jencks (1972) who, in a comprehensive, critical analysis of the American problem of social disadvantage, states that schools are unqualified to make the changes that would bring about equality of opportunity as long as the absolute level of inequality persists in society. The same is true in Britain . . .

That is the message of the 1970s. It is small wonder we are depressed, yet the interesting factor is that practitioners go on trying, believing, hoping and the academics go on designing ever newer forms of intervention. What is the reason for this? I am convinced that one reason concerns the kind of self-selected optimistic people we are ourselves; another is our basic assumption that all people have the capacity to change; the third is that sometimes intervention works and an individual child or adult or a family is seen to emerge from the swamp and join the rest of us. When this happens there are usually quite specific reasons which have not as yet been fully examined, but the fact that it can happen at all fits in with the mythology of our society that if you want to enough, you can do anything – another assumption we have to question.

Hauling the odd person out of the swamp still leaves the problem of what will happen to the many who are left. The more effective our selection and promotion procedures, the more important it becomes to consider the future of those who may be seen as permanently disadvantaged or poor.

Who are the rest of us?

Let us first look at the lives of those of us who are supposed to be the advantaged. We are the people who have successfully adapted to this urban, industrial, bureaucratic world. If we consider the poor to be trapped in their poverty perhaps we should consider that we too may be trapped in a different kind of cage – more comfortable perhaps, but still a cage.

From every research source there is a constant re-statement of the powerful way in which as individuals we are shaped by the human group in which we live; the formidable influence of home and neighbourhood on our values, attitudes and assumptions, the significance of the family as a transmitter of values from parents to children. In a stable society this transmission is relatively uniform from generation to generation and little choice of alternative futures or scenarios is made available.

For the advantaged, the traditional family has always had particular significance – it represents quite specific values of respect for authority, orderliness, hierarchy of age and responsibility, paternalism and mutual support. Yet less than a decade ago, within the advantaged group, passionate arguments were being put forward that far from being a 'good', the family structure was a kind of monster, the source of madness, of unhealthy dependencies, of sexual crippling. The work of Laing (1971) and Cooper (1971) explored family sickness in the context of a sick society, where the family served to impose conformity at the expense of self-realisation and creativity, where 'madness' became an escape into sanity (Laing, 1964, 1971; Cooper, 1971).

The function of the family to provide soldiers, salesmen and reinforcers of the existing order was challenged then because the children of the advantaged were challenging the nature of the society itself. The attack on the family went hand in hand with the emergence of student militancy, the drop-out movement, the gay movement, women's liberation and experiments in communal living.

The rebellion seemed not to last very long. It was another aspect of the expansionist 1960s. The university drop-outs knew that they could drop back in any time. The 1970s presents a very different picture. Student militancy has been replaced by sober, vocationally-directed students, few drop-outs, an institutionalised gay movement, a deeply confused women's movement and a resurgence of interest in the family.

The major political parties are emphasising family policy and are expressing a need to strengthen its traditional forms. There is a serious possibility that a minister for the family will be appointed who will be required to scrutinise all legislation for its implications for the family.

These parties traditionally represent the interests of advantaged groups and we have to ask ourselves what these interests are which are requiring reinforcement. The main interest is stability – to be able to maintain their advantage in a rapidly changing world. Rebelliousness has withdrawn from the middle class, and professional groups. They are settling down to weather out the storm. A different form may be focusing in the respectable working class who were virtually unaffected by the anti-family movement of the 1960s. They are the group who are going to be most sharply affected by the technological changes which are taking place around us. A car worker sitting at home watching a programme on automated factories is entitled to be edgy when no one is discussing alternative futures with him. He is near enough to the poor not to want to join them through unemployment. Strikes are a reflection of insecurity rather than security.

The middle class may not be correct in their assumption that they can survive the changes we face as a society. Their market skills were developed in response to the needs of the industrial society. Education developed 'subjects' in schools which in the adult world became 'careers' or 'professions'. Industry and management required techniques of dividing a process into its component parts. The process started when human beings were first attached to machines in factories.

> Reducing every man's business to some one simple operation, and by making this operation the sole employment of his life, necessarily increases very much the dexterity of the workman. (Smith, 1784)

The working-class humans became components of the machine, which is why they may be the first victims of the technical revolution;

the middle class have tried to master the machines by identifying with them and they have maintained some autonomy by power over others through their professional status. Many of us in the caring professions 'manage' the poor.

Children of either the middle or working classes who fitted neatly into the school machine have been allowed to graduate to professional or near professional status themselves. The first requirement for these children is that the school machine has to be seen as a 'good'. The children of the poorest families have rarely had that conviction.

The function of the schools is primarily to reproduce their professionals' image of what a society is about. This of course is based on their learned image of the market economy. Their first task is therefore to reproduce themselves as the core and then those who will be content with more humble and undemanding jobs. In 1979 it is still possible to hear teachers talking about building boredom in to the classroom situation because 'these children' will have to live with it in any job they may be lucky enough to get.

But the machines, like education, are changing, and the ways of managing them have to change too.

The strengths of the poor

The basic reason for the success of the middle class has been their loyal support for the values of the industrial society. These, as I have already said, are thrift, achievement, independence, endurance, self-control: they are the same values we have tried to teach the poor. The poor have, with some consistency, rejected them. What we have to ask ourselves is this: are these values relevant in the new society which is emerging?

There is a growing consensus that we have been in a post-industrial society for some years and that new forms of production of wealth are emerging with some rapidity. A basic assumption of the post-industrial society is that because of the advanced technology the production of economically required goods will no longer absorb the energies of most of the people. This irreversible trend has been known to us, but until recently it appeared that there would be plenty of time to prepare for it. It now appears that the trend is proceeding more rapidly and more unevenly than had been anticipated both within and between countries. It is already affecting decisions and people both consciously and unconsciously.

One specific, anticipated effect is the likelihood of very large numbers of unemployed. Estimates vary but all agree that it will be significant and will affect the majority of the population. It was originally thought that it would only affect the industrial worker but the unexpectedly fast development of uses for microprocessors means that it will strike quickly at service industries and a wide range of management skills. The group affected will be caught in unemployment with a set of values based on the work ethic which could be not only useless but actually damaging. Studies of the families of the unemployed consistently show depressive illnesses stemming from loss of self-respect as a major hazard. Minor consequences are insomnia, marital disharmony, behaviour problems among the children, an increased number of visits to the doctor.

As in most advanced societies certain parts of the economy are already in an early phase of post-industrialism, while many others are at an industrial stage and others may even be pre-industrial. With advanced communication, particularly television, consciousness of change is spreading without us having a framework into which we can place ourselves in the world we are entering. A period of turbulence is inevitable.

We may have to look to those poor people who have held on to the pre-industrial values for a guide to the emerging society for which some of us are so ill-equipped. Let us consider again what those may be – interdependence, spontaneity and the capacity for joy. These are all values we have seen put down by teachers, residential staffs, social workers, ministers, because the form in which they express themselves if often socially unacceptable: borrowing equals lack of thrift; spontaneity equals lack of self-control; capacity for joy equals lack of the capacity to endure.

Perhaps most difficult of all the core industrial values to abandon is that of achievement, since for the middle class achievement equals status which too often equals identity. Fromm (1976) identifies that as the problem of the post-industrial society. He argues that we are living in a time which requires radical changes in the attitudes and values of human beings. Joy has in the past been seen as something to be earned. Sadly the way of earning it has often destroyed the capacity to experience it.

Changes in values

But there has been movement already in ways that are important to understand. The sudden shift in values that took place in the 1960s can be seen as a foreshadowing of events that were beginning to take shape. The present retreat is perhaps temporary. One factor was the questioning of accepted authority, the 'new impertinence' as it was described by one sociologist. It was reflected in attitudes to medicine, education, the law, religion and politics by the rapidly expanding affluent working class, who gave momentum to the middle class. This process of bourgeoisification led to the consumer and participation developments of the 1970s.

In the general community there is a growing sense that the capacity to endure should no longer be necessary even for the poor. There seems to be no erosion of the idea that differentials should be maintained nor is it unacceptable that some people should be better off than others, but to be poor at this stage of the century is recognised as a due subject of complaint even for the unemployed. Their place in the queue for increases is clearly at the end but their right to queue is recognised. It can indeed be used as an argument by the low paid for improvement in their own condition.

The value of self-control has been exploded interestingly enough by the very money houses who needed the thrift ethic of the nineteenth century. The 'buy now' boom of the High Streets in the 1960s has been summed up in the Access card slogan 'take the waiting out of wanting'. The message is quite clear and crude. While it may bring together the values of the poor in whom spontaneity has a different meaning and the values of the more affluent, its intention is basically exploitative. That should not blind us to its longer-term significance.

At another and more interpersonal level, the concept of self-control in relationships confronted the technology of the oral contraceptive – and collapsed. To take a contraceptive as a pill could not be seen as sinful in a society which had already sanctioned the taking of pills for headaches, depression and anxiety. This links in with the capacity to endure. The development of chemotherapy after the Second World War had meant it was no longer necessary for the GP to tell his patients with emotional problems to pull themselves together. He could give them a tranquilliser or an antidepressant or a whole new range of drugs for physical illnesses. The idea gained ground that to every problem there was a solution. Scientific control seemed established and in consequence self-control was less necessary.

The welfare state had, quite deliberately, set itself the task of devaluing the belief in independence which had been such a cornerstone of the industrial society. The Poor Law had bitten so deeply and bitterly into the minds and imagination of the working class that the post-war Labour governments felt it necessary to exaggerate the right of every person paying contributions to a free health service and to benefits as of right without means testing. To encourage people to take welfare benefits without shame required constant exhortation and still does for the elderly. To cling to independence was described as false pride and the idea of mutual social support and interdependence was offered as a more moral stance. Families were not to be expected to cope alone with their young, their sick or their aged: community facilities were to be developed. This led in the late 1950s and early 1960s to the development of groups of every kind, therapeutic groups, consciousness-raising groups, encounter groups, communes. The individual and the individualistic nuclear family was out, the group was in.

More distressing for many people, and particularly for some parents, has been the loss in many sections of the young of the drive for achievement. The expansion of the universities had brought new-style, young, working-class people flooding into subjects like sociology and psychology seeking not vocational learning but trying desperately to make sense of their worlds. The post-Christian era had begun and they sought in these subjects alternative interpretations of their confusions. The impact of their questions swept through the whole generation. The goals of their parents who had been goaded by insecurity and ambition seemed petty and unworthy and they seemed to see little point in sacrificing present pleasures for uncertain futures. The effect of the bomb hung over all. Aldermaston became a great pre-industrial pagan procession and ritual.

All these changes in attitudes, as well as the ones I described earlier, sent shock waves through our society. For the first time the notion of alternative futures began to be discussed by young people. The alternative society was the world of being not having, of spontaneity, the capacity for joy, self-actualisation, self-expression. Much of the behaviour was childish and irresponsible, sometimes self-destructive, but much was beautiful, loving and creative. Behind slogans like 'make love not war' lay the kind of wisdom that only young and innocent people can achieve.

The notion of alternative societies was essentially about the quality of life and this went hand in hand with the development of groups concerned with ecology and conservation. For many it was their first questioning of the assumption that the prime duty of industry was to make profits. Attacking industry's right to pollute rivers, some critics thought, was a more important issue to the middle class than attacking industry's right to exploit immigrant workers at Grunwick's but everyone has to start where they are and the concept of an interdependent world was growing in different ways.

The world of the advantaged has in fact been preparing itself in some ways for the post-industrial society, but I would question whether it has done so sufficiently. We who are concerned with the poor are probably convinced that we will still have plenty of work to do; we may even assume that yet more of us will be needed if the numbers of the unemployed rise and become the new poor. We may even have in our heads some kind of image of the 1930s and the classical depression.

I would argue that this is no model for the future. No democratic society can be based on a small elite of workers, some of whom are producing wealth and some of whom are managing large numbers of poor.

Opportunities for change

If we do not change our styles of relating to and paying the unemployed that is what would happen. Families of long-term unemployed have the lowest income, the lowest standard of living and the lowest status of any group of families in the country. We have been able to contain them socially until now because they have not in fact grasped the irreversible nature of their situation. The previous hard core of the long-term unemployed have not accepted their role passively – as delinquency, truancy and vandalism figures show – but they have accepted their powerlessness. The new poor are not likely to do that. Already the young people leaving school without jobs are reacting more sharply against authority. This can only gain momentum if young people face the possibility of their future as being life on the dole.

Some professionals may be tempted to create new machines to manage the new problems in old ways. A report from the National Institute for Careers Education and Counselling has recommended teaching children the survival tactics of unemployment and drawing social security benefit. An important idea certainly, but not enough in itself. Our true task as professionals should be not to manage the machines but to change them. I am sure many of us have wanted to do this in any case but have not known how.

The excitement of the changes that are taking place is that it is going to be possible. The Chinese use an ideogram to represent the word crisis which means problem and opportunity linked. That is where we are now. Unfortunately for some, fear of an unknown future can prevent any rational anticipation of change. They will either bury their heads in the sand or stoutly resist. By perceiving change as always for the worse they fail to recognise the positive opportunities for growth and learning which always accompany change. Those of us who are advantaged have a greater responsibility to reach out for those positive opportunities so as to include the poor.

How can we change the machine?

The goal has to be create alternative futures for the poor, and particularly for poor parents and children as full members of our society. This means, as David Donnison (1975) has said, not only income, though that is central, but access to resources like health, education and housing on equal terms with everyone else, access to status and respect, participation in decision-making. We have to recognise that this has significant implications for the rest of us. It means also that they have to see themselves and be seen by others as making a contribution to that society.

The future of work

As yet the only way we know of making a clearly-identified contribution to society is by working and being paid for it. No matter how much we say we value voluntary work, no matter how many OBEs it attracts, it does not have the same meaning as doing work which is assessed by the community as necessary or important in some way, and significant to the life of the community. Those in our society who are not seen to contribute – children, students, the sick and handicapped, the dependent and the aged, along with the unemployed – are treated as less than full citizens. That may change some day but it will not change tomorrow.

What is going to change tomorrow is that there will be fewer jobs. This is a mixed blessing – as is all change. The good aspect is that the jobs which are disappearing are in many cases dull, uninteresting and soul-destroying; the bad aspect is that awful though they may have been they gave shape and purpose and a sense of meaning, no matter how false, to the lives of those who held them and to the lives of their families.

We, as a society, have a choice. We can relegate these workers to the ranks of the poor and talk about a leisure society and how we must educate people to live their lives without working – and we can wait for the consequences. On the other hand we can decide that the work that has to be done must be reallocated among everyone who wants to work and that the poor must not be written off as non-contributors. This may mean that we might only have to work one day a week or one day a year, but the significance lies in being included.

One argument currently being advanced is that the school leaving age should be raised and the retirement age lowered. I would think that our experience of the disenfranchised young and elderly argues against that if it means narrowing still further the band of those allowed to work. Rather I would suggest that the expectation of a contribution and the right to make a contribution should be extended down the age scale and up beyond the retirement age for all those who wish it. Our ruthless exclusion of children and the elderly from the market place has been well intentioned but has had unhappy consequences for many.

Leisure and income

It is easy to talk about a leisure society and preparing people for leisure but it is more difficult to achieve. Industrialism has drained many people of their natural capacities for creativity and self-actualisation.

A key factor will have to be a change in our present style of differentials in income. This again is a direct consequence of industrialism, and the subtle and not so subtle use of a little more money as an inducement to take on more work or more responsibility. It differentiates between the skilled and the unskilled and is a cornerstone of the achievement ethic. It is also a deep source of division between workers. The differential has become a deeply embedded status system which no one seems to challenge. It is reflected in a hundred ways – the infinite variety of houses and house prices is one example, but perhaps the motor car shows it up most sharply and in its greatest absurdity. We produce a wide range of motor cars – all to serve the same basic function of transporting groups of between one and at the most five people from one place to another, but each subtly different in style and price so as to identify precisely the owner's income range and status.

A leisure society for all cannot grow with intolerable differences existing in pay and living standards between different groups. The very opportunities that leisure creates will stimulate demand for resources. This has already happened even with the five-day week; one example is the way in which co-ownership of yachts has brought sailing down the social scale to the working class. People who become unemployed are not going to be willing to abandon their newly discovered pleasures. A whole leisure industry has been built around them. This also applies to the pay of those unable to work. We must stop talking and thinking about benefits and think in terms of pay for everyone whether they are in or out of work. This includes school children and the retired as well as the sick and disabled. The single parent bringing up children obviously earns his or her pay, as do children at school. We have to offer opportunities imaginatively to all other groups to do the same. Everyone has something to offer. The one thing no one can say is that there is any shortage of needs for carers in our society. What we will need to face is whether we need as many 'professionals' as we have.

Power

Power has to be shared. For the professionals amongst us this is perhaps the most difficult future to envisage since it involves our own roles and self-esteem; yet if we have any skills and if we wish to change the machines which we help to manage, this is where we have most opportunity to do so.

Communities and groups, particularly poor ones, must be given the right to manage their own affairs whenever possible. The consumer and participation movements of the 1970s to which I referred earlier excluded the poor, who have had to rely consistently for a voice in the committee rooms on those professionals whose career has involved speaking for the poor. Of course, local authority services pay lip service to the participation of those who live in the poorest areas. The officials make sincere but incomprehensible gestures which appear to offer little conviction and show little reality in the resultant decision-making.

Yet, for those who choose to hear, community groups particularly of the poor have consistently demonstrated their understanding of the dilemmas of their own life. One such group is the Craigmillar Festival Society. Craigmillar is a suburb of Edinburgh and a classical area of multiple deprivation. The title of the group is an ironic comment on the elite and expensive Edinburgh Festival. It grew out of the frustration of a mother whose son wanted to learn the violin but whose school's attitude was 'it takes us all our time to teach these children the three Rs far less music'. In response a group of mothers organised an annual festival, and this proved to be the key that unlocked the creative talents within the community and became a base for a massive programme of social action. It was run initially on a purely voluntary basis then on Urban Aid, and now as part of an EEC Poverty Programme. It now has twenty full-time staff, mostly local residents, and is responsible for a wide range of community welfare activities as well as job creation, an art resource centre, environmental improvement and a bi-monthly newspaper.

No professional initiative has been so successful except perhaps in a different way in the Australian experiment run by the Brotherhood of St Laurence in Melbourne and the Family Centre Project (Liffman, 1978). Here a group of the most deprived families were imaginatively helped to develop an anti-poverty community programme run by themselves for themselves. It involved a conscious decision on the part of the professionals to withdraw entirely from the decision-making process. Like Craigmillar, the emphasis has been on income, jobs and social action.

We can learn something from China where the neighbourhood committee run by the residents of housing projects take responsibility for preventive health programmes, vandalism prevention, the promotion of good social relationships along with protection and preservation of the environment. Because they have never had professionals to do these things for them they make a particularly interesting focus for study. There may be some specialist skills needed but that is a different matter. One group who are particularly open to these kinds of ventures are the parents of young children, since they can be involved in their children's future which can seem to offer more promise than their own ever gave. There seems to be a critical point when that belief blossoms, but if not met it fades.

These techniques of standing back to enable creativity to develop will be as important with the newly displaced. For them, areas of autonomy will be essential as they adjust to new roles. As their sense of having power is withdrawn from the workplace it will be increasingly important that they should feel they have a voice and are valued in the political decision-making processes.

An even more obvious area for these developments is the field of education. It is already under severe scrutiny, many observers believing that schools by their very structure have become the source of alienation and disaffection in the young: they seem increasingly to select out rather than bring in. The changing social climate is going to be unmapped territory for teachers as much as for everyone else. Their ideas about appropriate subjects and curriculum planning are going to require radical reassessment. This is already beginning among the more aware. It seems an obvious time to abandon defensive postures and involve parents in the puzzling times ahead. Being free of the assumptions of the educational system, this is one occasion when the disadvantaged may have even more to offer than the advantaged if we can listen to them. Precisely because the advantaged have been successful they tend to live in yesterday's world.

The processes I am describing are not going to be easy to achieve. They require confidence that all people are capable of being involved in the future and of making a contribution. It will take time to make such a path and there could be many problems to face on the way. One response to change can be vandalism and disorder on a scale we have not yet experienced. Gramsci (1971) wrote about social change: 'The crisis consists precisely in the fact that the old is dying and the new cannot be born: in this interregnum a great variety of morbid symptoms appears.' We have to see these responses as signs of vitality, a refusal to accept docilely the humiliating and degrading expectations of a powerful, small social caucus. A nation of depressed poor people might be less obviously disruptive but it would be much more sick.

Conclusion

The thoughts I am trying to convey are complex, incompletely thought out and open to misinterpretation. I do not apologise for that. This is a time for us to take chances, try out ideas and welcome criticism which may take our thinking a step forward into the future. The essence of my message is that we can have alternative futures. The future is not decided in advance, we are continually making it. We are currently entering a rare open moment in history, a space into which we can insert our wills.

The Industrial Revolution was one such: it did not need to happen with such cruelty and ruthless pursuit of profit. Some parts of the country are still paying a sore price for that. It is not a coincidence that these are also the areas of our greatest deprivation. We must see that our current Technological Revolution does not repeat those mistakes.

In fact those of us concerned with the existence of the poor have a particular opportunity to achieve those goals we have sought in our professional lives. There need no longer be an acceptance and recognition of the poor as a permanent feature of urban societies. We can work with change not only to abolish poverty but to understand that the poor have a great deal to teach us about living, as neither parts of the machines of work nor managers of those machines. We may learn to be ourselves and by sharing the world with them enrich all our lives.

But it has to be a new world with new values. Our world and our values are dying, a new world and new yet old values struggling to be born. It will be painful for those of us who have been privileged, we may not like some of the new and we will have to question many of our activities from which we have derived our status and self-esteem. We will be forced to live up to our private belief that we are loving and caring people.

The revolution is taking place not only in Britain but all over the world. We are part of a great process. It is important that we influence it.

Bibliography

Central Advisory Council for Education (1967) *Children and Their Primary Schools* (Plowden Report) (London: HMSO).

Committee on Local Authority and Allied Personal Social Services (1968) *Report of the Committee* (Seebohm Report) (London: HMSO).

Cooper, D. (1971) *The Death of the Family* (London: Allen Lane).

Department of Education and Science (1974a) *Educational Priority vol. 1. EPA: Problems and Policies*, ed. A. H. Halsey (London: HMSO).

Department of Education and Science (1974b) *Educational Priority. vol. 2 EPA surveys and statistics*, by J. Payne (London: HMSO).

Donnison, D. (1975) *An Approach to Social Policy* (National Economic and Social Council Paper no. 8) (Dublin: Stationery Office).

Fromm, E. (1976) *To Have Or To Be* (New York: Harper and Row).

Gramsci, A. (1971) *Prison Notebooks* (London: Lawrence and Wishart).

Jencks, C. (1972) *Inequality* (New York: Basic Books).

Laing, R. D. (1971) *The Politics of the Family and Other Essays* (London: Tavistock Publications).

Laing, R. D. and Esterson, A. (1964) *Sanity, Madness and the Family* (London: Tavistock Publications).

Liffman, M. (1978) *Power for the Poor* (London: Allen and Unwin).

Smith, A. (1776) *Wealth of Nations*, 3rd ed 1976 (Oxford University Press).

Watts, A. G. (1979) *The Implications of School Leaver Unemployment for Careers Education in Schools* (NICEC Occasional paper no. 1) (Cambridge: Research and Advisory Centre).

Wilson, H. and Herbert, G. W. (1978) *Parents and Children in the Inner City* (London: Routledge and Kegan Paul).

7

Promoting Good Child Health

F. S. W. Brimblecombe

Contemporary society has moved a long way from the era when it naively believed that further major improvements in child health must wait for new discoveries in science and medicine. This basic truth is nowhere better illustrated than at the present time in developing countries in Africa and Asia where the malignant influence of the combination of childhood malnutrition and infectious disease still causes the deaths of at least half the whole childhood population before their fifth birthday. Yet our scientific knowledge of childhood nutrition is theoretically more than sufficient to eliminate malnutrition, as are the methods to prevent most of the common infectious diseases.

The reasons why this existing knowledge is not applied are complex, stemming as they do from deep-rooted cultural influences and religious beliefs, critical economic factors which cause the perpetuation of poverty and the failure to utilise improved technology in agriculture and food production, lack of educational and health services and the administrative organisation of services which even in the presence of limited resources could be made far more effective than those that presently exist. Above all there is a lack of motivation among human beings both inside and outside the Third World to work together to transform a situation which is clearly identified and potentially remediable.

In industrial societies like our own, the need to improve the health, education and care of our children is as urgent as in the Third World although the particular problems and unmet needs are very different. In many instances the remedies are available and the reasons why they are not applied are as complex as those in the Third World.

Childhood deaths

If I start by using childhood deaths as an example, it is because mortality statistics provide reasonably reliable measurements. Nevertheless the principles involved apply to almost every aspect of child health and care.

Social class

In Britain, social class differences despite a trend towards the levelling of net income between trades and professions, still reveal dramatic differences in infant mortality rates (see Tables 7.1 and 7.2). In Sweden and Finland the horrifying social class mortality gradient so apparent in these Scottish figures (which apply equally to other parts of the United Kingdom) are almost non-existent, except for the experience of illegitimate infants in whom the infant death rates are proportionately far greater than in the rest of the child population. The reasons for this wide variation in infant death rates between different socio-economic groups in Britain are not susceptible to

TABLE 7.1   *Infant mortality rates by social class, Scotland compared with Sweden and Finland*

Social class	Mortality rates (deaths per 1000 live born infants)		
	Neonatal (first month)	Post-neonatal (one month to one year)	Infant (under one year)
Scotland (1972)			
I	7.5	2.7	10.2
II	9.4	4.0	13.4
III	12.3	5.8	18.1
IV	12.6	7.5	20.1
V	15.5	12.0	27.5
Sweden (1974)			
All social classes	7.5	2.0	9.5
Finland (1973)			
All social classes	8.3	1.7	10.0

TABLE 7.2   *Low birthweight by social class, UK 1970 (British births, 1970)*

Social class	Percentage of births 2500 g and less	Percentage of births 3000 g and less
I, II	4.5	19.0
III	5.6	23.7
IV, V	8.2	27.3
Single, widowed or divorced	9.5	33.3

simple explanation; indeed, the reasons are as multifactorial as those related to the high childhood mortality in developing countries. Before attempting to identify some of them, I wish to make some further comparisons between different groups both within Britain and with some other European countries.

Birth weight

It is well recognised that infant mortality and especially neonatal mortality rates are closely correlated with birth weight. Thus a population which has a relatively higher proportion of low birth weight infants within it will have a higher proportion of neonatal and infant deaths. To summarise a mass of data, three main trends emerge in England. First, there is a significantly higher proportion of low birth weight infants in the north of England than in the south. Second, throughout England the large towns and conurbations have a higher proportion of low birth weight infants than is found in rural areas. Third, and certainly associated with the first two trends, low birth weight is closely correlated with variations in social class. The actual survival rates of low birth weight infants in the north of England compared with the south, and in the large towns and conurbations compared with rural areas, show only minor differences. It is the higher proportion of low birth weight babies in the north and in the urban areas which accounts for much of the variation in the infant mortality rates in different parts of this country. When the birth statistics of these various populations are standardised for birth weight much, but not all, of the differences between them are greatly reduced.

Extent of differences in perinatal and infant death rates between areas of England

The information derived from studies of social class and birth weight variations are not of themselves sufficient to account for the differences in infant death rates. These wide local variations that still exist in England are illustrated by identifying the areas of England which had the widest differences in 1976 (see Tables 7.3 and 7.4). These local variations, which occur not only between areas of England but actually within individual precincts of particular cities, suggest differences not only in socio-economic status as defined by the occupation of the father but also both in the life-style (including attitudes to child-rearing) within communities and in the services available to families with children (housing, town planning, recreational facilities for children, health, educational and social services for both children and their families).

TABLE 7.3 *Local perinatal mortality rates, England, 1976 (stillbirths and first-week deaths per 1000 total births)*

Area of England	Perinatal mortality rate
England	17.6
Dudley	23.7
Rochdale	22.9
Barnsley	22.4
Suffolk	12.0
Camden and Islington	11.0
Oxfordshire	10.4

TABLE 7.4 *Local infant mortality rates, England, 1976 (deaths under one year of age per 1000 live births)*

Area of England	Infant mortality rate
England	14.2
Rochdale	20.7
Wolverhampton	20.5
Bury	10.6
Oxfordshire	10.1

Some international comparisons

International comparisons of childhood mortality in six West
European countries reveal interesting contrasts between them (see
Tables 7.5 and 7.6). A breakdown of these figures into particular
causes of death in this age group is also revealing, if they are divided
into mainly preventable and mainly non-preventable groups. The

TABLE 7.5   *Infant mortality rates in Western
European countries, 1971 (deaths under one year
of age per 1000 live births)*

Country	Infant mortality rate
Sweden	11.1
Holland	11.4
France	16.0
England and Wales	17.2
Belgium	20.5
West Germany	23.5

TABLE 7.6   *Deaths of children aged 1–4 years
per 100 000 population, 1972*

Country	All causes
Sweden	42.0
England and Wales	70.5
France	79.0
Holland	83.0
Belgium	87.0
West Germany	95.0

countries which have the highest percentage of deaths due to
currently non-preventable causes can be considered to have the best
performance, whilst countries with the highest percentages due to
preventable causes are those in which there is greatest room for
improvement (see Tables 7.7, 7.8 and 7.9).

TABLE 7.7   *Percentages of deaths of children aged 1–4 years per 100 000 population from different causes, 1972*

Country	Neoplasms and congenital malformations (mainly non-preventable)	Accidents (mainly preventable)	Infections (mainly preventable)
Sweden	**40.4**	**26.4**	**7.2**
England and Wales	28.6	27.5	*18.1*
Holland	24.8	*38.8*	10.8
West Germany	23.7	33.0	12.6
Belgium	20.6	30.7	12.8
France	*17.5*	32.6	10.0

Bold type indicates good performance; *italic* type indicates poor performance.

TABLE 7.8   *Deaths of children aged 5–14 years per 100 000 population, 1972*

Country	All causes
Sweden	32.3
England and Wales	33.7
Holland	37.9
France	38.6
Belgium	42.1
West Germany	45.7

Health services for children

Valid comparisons of services for children among Western European countries must be multidisciplinary in nature and command a degree of knowledge beyond my competence. I can only attempt to comment on certain differences between the pattern of the maternity services and the child health services for children of pre-school age in some countries.

In Finland, child health nurses, and in Sweden, public health nurses, play a key role in both these services. Practically the whole infant population (99 per cent) is in regular contact with these nurses

TABLE 7.9   *Percentages of deaths in children aged 5–14 years per 100 000 population from different causes, 1972*

Country	Neoplasms and congenital malformations (mainly non-preventable)	Accidents (mainly preventable)	Infections (mainly preventable)
Sweden	**33.9**	38.9	3.6
England and Wales	29.6	**37.8**	*7.1*
Belgium	23.1	48.0	4.5
Holland	22.5	*51.2*	**3.5**
West Germany	21.5	48.5	**3.5**
France	*20.8*	44.2	3.8

Bold type indicates good performance; *italic* type indicates poor performance.

both through home visits and at child health centres. In Finland, the initial role of the child health nurse is to establish contact with the family in the antenatal period. At this early stage of child-rearing, not only is the medical obstetric and nursing midwifery service involved, but the child health nurse begins to establish her own relationship with each new family. Her initial objective is to become known by them as a friendly adviser who will become increasingly involved with their preparation for parenthood in all its aspects and later as the named person whom they will feel able to consult informally after the birth of the baby. During this antenatal stage, an experienced child health nurse will learn to identify those families in her district whose social and emotional characteristics indicate that they are likely later on to need a high level of support as child-rearers.

After the birth of the baby, the medical profession in much of Scandinavia have come to rely upon child health or public health nurses to provide most of the front-line primary child health care. The parents may consult the nurse by telephone, at the child health centre or at a home visit about any child health problem that confronts them at any time. The matter may be technically a trivial or a serious one, but whatever its nature, it will provide the nurse with further insight into the capability of the family. She can use minor problems as an opportunity to give the family the appropriate confidence and skill to deal with situations with her support. For more serious problems, she can advise a consultation with the family doctor, the hospital, the psychiatric service or the social worker.

It is important to emphasise that this does not preclude direct consultation between the parents and the family doctor but provides easy, informal and immediate access to professional help. Minor problems which the nurse (who is often the person best qualified to advise about them) deals with herself are rapidly identified; more serious conditions are brought to appropriate expert professional attention at a very early stage in their development, so that medical, psychiatric or social care can be mobilised before the situation has reached serious proportions. Thus in Scandinavia the relationship between the family and the nurse, which comes to contain many of the best elements of partnership, continues throughout the early years of childhood.

It is one of the strengths of this service that the child health or public health nurse participates not only in preventive but also in any curative home nursing that may be needed. On average there are twelve contacts between these nurses and the family during the child's first year of life, of which three or four are home visits. In Britain, the average number of home visits is one per annum. This figure refers to children born during one year and does not therefore treat all children the same as it includes those born at various times during the calendar year.

In summary, Scandinavian children have more contact with their health service than do British children. With no disrespect to our own health visitors, Scandinavian child health and public health nurses are better placed to provide the type of service needed by a young family with a small child than is the pattern of service usually available in this country. This is because of their relatively greater numbers, the nature of their training, their concentrated attention upon families with young children and their delegated responsibility within the primary health care service both for preventive and curative care. Yet despite this provision, Dr Claus Sunderlin found in his recent survey in Uppsala in Sweden that parents are so aware of the importance of this type of service that they requested 'increased access to advice from nurses for example on the telephone, by more evening sessions at child health centres, more help with nursing sick children, longer sessions with doctors when there are serious problems, more and better advice on problems of child behaviour and better premises for child health centres'. This from a country which has one of the best child health records in the world!

Child health needs in Britain

I have concentrated my examples upon childhood mortality, but comparable information is becoming available about childhood illness. Prevention of childhood handicap goes hand in hand with prevention of child mortality. In the face of the evidence concerning British perinatal and infant mortality the DHSS's claim (1976) that 'the hospital maternity services have attracted too large a share of our resources; and that the minimum aim should be to have lowered their cost by about 7 per cent by 1979/80' is almost impossible to comprehend. In France, it has been made illegal for a maternity hospital to be licensed unless there are adequate facilities for the effective conduct of the birth process, resuscitation of the newborn and staff properly trained to use them. Regretfully, there are many maternity hospitals in this country which do not fulfil these criteria.

The stated intention in the same DHSS document, to strengthen our primary health care teams by an increase in the number of health visitors and home nurses, is welcome. There is no evidence, however, that this will result in any extra concentration of specialised community nurses for children (as exists in Scandinavia); the elderly, the physically handicapped and children are listed as the main target areas upon which this group of generically orientated nurses will be directed.

Fit for the Future, the Court Report (DHSS, 1976), tells a very different story. The first volume of the report provides a far more comprehensive account of the child health needs of children than I could possibly attempt here. For example, I have only just touched on the high number of preventable deaths from infection in infancy and early childhood in Britain compared with all other Western European countries. I have only just mentioned the enormous problems posed by accidents to children both in their homes and by road accidents; whilst statistics suggest that the childhood accident situation in this country is as satisfactory as anywhere in Western Europe, it would be criminal to be complacent. I have not even mentioned the enormous potential for prevention of dental disease in childhood (for which all the necessary knowledge is available – if only we had the will and motivation to use it).

The Court Report provided a radical and imaginative plan for the future although it advised that the resource implications of their recommendations meant that this plan would take 15 to 20 years to achieve. Nearly three of these years have slipped by. One recommendation, however, which has now been implemented is the formation of 'The Children's Committee'. The report asked the question: 'Whose job will it be to see that any of our recommendations that are accepted are actually carried out? Not just as elegantly worded circulars of advice and direction but actually in surgeries and clinics, hospitals, schools and homes. And in the spirit we intended? There seemed to be no group we could ask to take this on.' They recommended the formation of a Children's Committee, which should be a group of not more than twelve to fourteen individuals appointed not as representatives of particular professions, but with a composition to ensure that knowledge of the personal social services, education and health services would be available. The strength of the Children's Committee was intended to lie and now exists in its right to give advice directly to the Secretaries of State for Social Services and for Wales. Its terms of reference are 'to advise the Secretaries of State on the co-ordination and development of health and personal social services as they relate to children and families with children'.

The total needs of children

I have concentrated on the need to improve child health in this country by means of prevention. In this final section, I wish to broaden this perspective to a consideration of the wider needs of children. I am starting my job as the first Chairman of this new Children's Committee with the conviction that we have in this country the potential to provide the finest child health, education and care service in the world. As some of my examples regarding child health have shown, in many respects we are a long way from that objective. Where we fall short I believe that the blame should be widely shared.

No central government in this country has yet made the type of commitment to its children that was made by the French government in 1971 or the Japanese government in 1974. No doubt both of these imaginative policy documents were the result of deep consideration by many agencies before they were promulgated as government policy. Perhaps in this country we have failed in our duty to alert successive central governments to the need to state 'their belief that children have special needs and rights which they cannot articulate for themselves and that society has therefore a duty to ensure that these are identified and cogently represented' (The Court Report, DHSS, 1976).

Like so many craft groups in contemporary society, professional bodies concerned with children (doctors, nurses, therapists, psychologists, teachers, social workers and some voluntary agencies) have become so preoccupied with their own status that they have lost sight of their primary function – service to children. Service means more than words and talk; to be genuine, service must show itself in action – the best servants are those to whom their own community accords the privilege of full membership, respect and partnership.

Is it perhaps necessary to remind some professionals of the words of Mannheim in 1936 about the dangers of ideology?

> The concept ideology reflects the one discovery which emerged from political conflict, namely that ruling groups can, in their thinking, become so intensively interest bound to a situation that they are simply no longer able to see certain facts which would undermine their sense of domination. This is implicit in the word ideology, the insight that in certain situations the collective unconsciousness of certain groups obscures the real condition of society both to itself and to others and thereby stabilizes it.

Much of the objections to the Court Report recommendations came from professional groups who objected to changes in their own roles and status. Their discussions in some cases contained little consideration of the total needs of children.

Above all, I believe that society as a whole needs to become aware of the urgent importance of giving a higher priority than has been given in the past to all aspects of child-rearing. This means an enhancement in the eyes of society of the needs of families with young children – through improved fiscal provision, consideration of the terms and conditions of employment of parents with young children, more effective provision for pre-school children in the form of better and more flexible child-minding, playgroup and nursery school facilities, and more accessible health and social work advice about the needs of children including family advice centres. More attention, in town planning and housing provision, needs to be given to the special needs of children.

All this can, I believe, be achieved if a catalytic process can develop and gain momentum which involves society at all levels (including central and local government, professional organisations, voluntary agencies and the general public at large) which will give the family with young children a far higher priority as a vital group in society charged with the responsibility of giving the new generation of children of this country the opportunity to achieve their full potential.

Bibliography

Brimblecombe, F. S. W., Ashford, J. R. and Fryer, J. G. (1968) 'Significance of low birthweight in perinatal mortality: a study of variations in England and Wales', *British Journal of Preventive and Social Medicine*, vol. 22, no. 1, pp. 27–35.

Chalmers, I., Newcombe, R., West, R., Campbell, H., Weatherall, J., Lambert, P. and Adelstein, A. (1978) 'Adjusted perinatal mortality rates in administrative areas of England and Wales,' *Health Trends*, vol. 10, no. 2, pp. 24–8.

Chalmers, I. (1978) *Perinatal Epidemiology* (London: Royal College of Obstetricians and Gynaecologists).

Chamberlain, R., Chamberlain, G., Howlett, B. and Claireaux, A. (1975) *British Births*, vol. 1 *The First Week of Life* (London: Heinemann Medical).

Children and Families Bureau (1974) *A Brief Report on Welfare Services in Japan* (Tokyo: Ministry of Health and Welfare).

Department of Health and Social Security (1976) *Priorities for Health and Personal Social Services in England* (London: HMSO).

Department of Health and Social Security and Child Poverty Action Group (1978) *Reaching the Consumer in the Antenatal and Child Services*, Report of Conference, 4 April 1978 (London: DHSS).

Department of Health and Social Security (1976) *Fit for the Future* (Court Report) (London: HMSO).

Economie et Santé (1973) *Le Bilan Avantage-Côsts des Dépistages Systématiques de Handicaps dans la Petite Enfance* (Paris).

Falkner, R. (1977) *Fundamentals of Mortality Risks During the Perinatal Period and Infancy* (Basel: Karger) (Monographs in Paediatrics, 9).

McLachlan, G. (ed.) (1975) *Bridging in Health* (Oxford University Press).

Mannheim, K. (1936) *Ideology and Utopia* (London: Routledge and Kegan Paul).

Ministère de la Santé Publique (1971) *Pour une politique de la Santé*, vol. 1 (Paris: Documentation Française).

Sundelin, C. (1973) 'Parents' experiences of child health centers.' *Scandinavian Journal of Social Medicine*, vol. 1, no. 3, pp. 133–47.

Vowles, M., Pethybridge, R. J. and Brimblecombe, F. S. W. (1975) 'Congenital malformations in Devon; their incidence, age and primary source of detection', In G. McLachlan, (ed.) *Bridging in Health* (Oxford University Press).

Wynn, M. and Wynn, A. (1976a) *Prevention of Handicap of Perinatal Origin* (London: Foundation for Education and Research in Child-Bearing).

Wynn, M. and Wynn, A. (1976b) *Paediatric Community Nursing* (Moor Park conference: Spastics Society).

8

Promoting School Adjustment

Ronald Davie

Disruptive behaviour, truancy and the like, especially in secondary schools, are perhaps some of the most worrying aspects of the current educational scene and, because of their association with delinquency, vandalism and with the 'Great Debate' about educational standards, this concern is widely shared. However, there is much uncertainty and confusion not only about the extent and nature of the problems but also about what, if anything, can be done to deal with, or to prevent, such behaviour.

Can schools have a preventive role?

When we look at the possibilities for preventive action – or any other action – by schools, we have first to ask: Does what the schools do make much, if any, difference anyway? A few examples will illustrate the reasons for this question: by and large, children do not come to school at all until after five years of age and the evidence on the importance for children of the first five years is well known; schools have no control over the emotional climate in homes, which is so important in children's development; schools cannot produce two parents where there is only one; schools cannot alter the physical conditions under which children live; schools cannot produce jobs in areas of high unemployment; neither can they increase the number of education welfare officers, psychologists, psychiatrists, speech therapists, remedial teachers, probation officers or social workers, where there are shortages.

Apart from a relatively few individual cases, then, can schools have any real effect upon children's behaviour or adjustment? Or even upon their educational attainments? Or is the school's influence, at least for any preventive action, narrowly confined within the straight-jacket imposed by external factors over which it has little or no control? Many teachers believe that this is the case. When faced with poor progress or unsatisfactory behaviour, 'What else can you expect', they say, 'when a substantial minority of children come from broken homes, or from large families with feckless, indifferent parents?' And in taking this view, teachers have seemed to have some measure of support from research evidence, usually from large-scale samples. This has indicated that the effects of home circumstances (notably parental interest and attitudes, but also housing conditions, family size, etc.) upon children's progress in school heavily outweigh any effects of school factors such as school size or type, class size, experience of staff, etc. (for example, Peaker, 1967; Wiseman, 1967).

This weight of evidence on the limited influence of schools seems strong. It comes, on the one hand, from experienced practitioners and on the other hand from disinterested, objective research. But this has to be set against other – I would suggest stronger – evidence that what individual schools and teachers do, and how they do it, does make a difference. Strangely, this contrary evidence comes from identical sources, that is, from practitioners and from research findings.

Every head teacher and experienced teacher knows that some of his colleagues are more effective than others – not only in terms of academic results but also in relation to the behaviour and adjustment of their pupils. Similarly every HMI, every local education authority adviser, every director and assistant director of education, every EWO, probably every local authority education committee member knows that some schools seem able to do a better job than others, even after allowance is made for different catchment areas. Indeed, it would be surprising if this were not the case since it is a common experience in every occupation that there are considerable differences in skill or effectiveness between the best and the worst. And such differences extend to institutions: we all know of shops, of firms, of colleges, even of local authority departments, which are more efficient, or more considerate, or more forward-looking than others.

Evidence on the influence of schools

In education the crucial issue is whether differences between schools are marginal and relatively unimportant, or whether what schools do and how they do it, really matters for their pupils. What is the research evidence to support the latter view? Leaving aside the question of academic results and of educational underfunctioning as such, I shall briefly consider the evidence that how schools manage their affairs can make a difference in terms of absenteeism from school, delinquency and in behaviour disorders. Then I will outline what might be done in terms of prevention.

This whole topic is very sensitive, as becomes apparent when the publication of external examination results for individual schools prompts comparisons. Undoubtedly this sensitivity is in large measure responsible for the paucity of research with this focus. However, an increasing number of schools are beginning to take a really professional attitude in this matter and are allowing researchers to examine school differences in order to learn more about the extent and nature of the differences and about the factors which lie behind them.

The evidence from a number of studies points to the fact that there are quite substantial differences in the behaviour and adjustment of pupils from different schools, which it seems cannot be accounted for in terms of the school intake or the catchment area. Thus, one enquiry in a London borough showed that amongst the twenty secondary modern schools they studied, the delinquency rate, averaged over five years, varied from less than 1 per 100 boys (aged 10 to 14 years) to 19 per 100 boys. These differences were not the initial focus of interest for the researchers, but they concluded after examining a wide range of other factors that some schools seemed to be notably better than others at preventing delinquent behaviour (Power *et al.*, 1972).

Two other projects, also carried out in London, reached similar conclusions, one in terms of child guidance referrals (Gath, 1972) and the other in relation to widely varying rates of 'psychiatric disorder' in schools, which could not be explained by external factors (Rutter, 1973).

The fourth study, undertaken in South Wales (Reynolds, 1977), looked at school absenteeism and delinquency in nine secondary modern schools in a mining valley, which is very homogeneous in terms of its social mix. It found, for example, that over a six-year period the average attendance in one school was 77 per cent and in another 89 per cent. The delinquency rate for pupils in these nine schools ranged from 4 per cent to 11 per cent; and the percentage of children going on to the local technical school ranged from 8 per cent to 53 per cent. Therefore it is reasonable to assume not only that individual teachers matter but that individual schools have an important part to play in preventing disruptive behaviour and delinquency, as well as in promoting good attendance and good motivation.

It is also reasonable to argue that the role of schools goes beyond that of identifying children at risk at an early stage and taking appropriate action. It extends to the active promotion of good adjustment and a positive attitude to schooling and to education. So much, then, for the evidence.

Methods of promoting adjustment

How do the best schools achieve their preventive influence? And how can we learn from them? This is a formidably difficult problem, which education shares with all other services. How can the elements of good practice be isolated? How can people be encouraged to change their way of working, to modify their attitudes, alter their style of thinking? How can good practice be promoted?

Traditional strategies for achieving this would include the dissemination of research reports and descriptive accounts in books and journals. But how many practitioners read such reports? Another well-used strategy is in-service training, which may take the form of 'one-off' conferences or extended courses.

The problems with these familiar strategies are threefold. First, they tend to reach a minority of people and these are often 'the converted'. Second, these strategies tend (if anything) to change what people know rather than what they do. Third, even when they influence what individuals do, they are likely to have minimal impact upon the system, upon the framework, upon the institution within which people work. And the constraints imposed by the institution will tend to block or frustrate efforts by individuals to develop or sustain new methods of working.

The question therefore becomes: how can institutional change be promoted? How can people, collectively, be encouraged to examine their objectives carefully, assess whether or to what extent these objectives are being achieved and, where necessary, to try out and evaluate new strategies?

There are as yet no clear answers to these questions, although much can be learned from attempts in factories, hospitals, etc., to promote good management and to improve labour relations.

A new strategy for promoting prevention

In South-east Wales we are about to launch a scheme to tackle this issue in schools, with particular reference to the promotion of good adjustment and the prevention of behaviour problems, truancy, poor motivation, learning difficulties and the like.

Last summer my colleagues and I in the Education Department of the University College, Cardiff, entered into discussions with the three neighbouring local education authorities (LEAs) (South and Mid Glamorgan and Gwent) on the topic of in-service training for teachers to deal with the above problems in secondary schools. We quickly came to two conclusions. First, school-based in-service training and staff development was likely to be the most effective strategy. Second, whatever we devised should somehow be directed at individual schools rather than at individual teachers. Unlike traditional in-service training, therefore, it would not be concerned with advancing the professional skills of individual teachers (as a primary objective). Rather it should aim to help schools to help themselves.

With this in mind a scheme was devised in collaboration with the three local authorities and in consultation with the head teachers of the secondary schools. It is geared to the needs of those teachers who have responsibility for pastoral care, for discipline (in some cases) and for school organisation and staff development in the areas of disruptive, difficult or deviant behaviour and truancy and the learning difficulties which are often associated with such behaviour.

At the centre of this scheme is a two-year university-based course in the Education Department, which can be pursued either in the context of a B.Ed. or an M.Ed. degree, depending on the prior qualifications of the teachers. It has been agreed with the head teachers that each will nominate for the course a senior colleague with the kind of responsibilities outlined above: someone with energy and initiative, whose judgement the headteacher trusts and whose voice will be listened to in the staff room.

Present indications are that a substantial majority of the 100 or so secondary schools in the three authorities want to take part; and the first thirty teachers started the course in October 1978 (five head teachers, twenty deputies or heads of school and five senior year tutors). They are being released from school for a half-day per week and are also attending for an evening. My colleagues and I have stressed to the participating teachers that they have as much, if not more, to learn from each other as they have from us and the visiting speakers.

The aims of the course are centred on helping the schools to ask the right questions rather than our trying to provide definitive answers. This is partly because we do not know too many of the answers yet and those that we do know need interpretation in the light of the particular circumstances of each school. More importantly, answers which a school works out for itself are more likely not only to be right but also to be implemented. Of course, we shall be carefully examining a wide range of strategies, but none of these is likely to provide ready-made solutions.

It would be misleading to present the situation as one in which South Wales schools are 'rising enthusiastically to the challenge of a bold and imaginative venture in prevention'. Head teachers – and especially their senior colleagues – are realists; some are sceptics (or even cynics). However, the majority of the heads – and certainly the LEAs – see this scheme as a constructive and positive step to help schools with a range of problems which are of considerable concern to them.

There is little doubt that over the two years of the course, the participating teachers will change. They will grow in understanding and they will be able to look at the problems from different points of view. Our discussions together will cover a wide range of issues: co-operation with social workers, doctors, psychologists and others; the relevance of the curriculum, particularly to academically less able children; home–school relations. And this wider understanding will lead to new ideas from the participating teachers for preventing problems arising and for dealing with them when they do arise.

What is less sure is the extent to which these teachers will be able to carry their schools along with them and how they will be able to share this new understanding with their colleagues. A consideration of these latter problems, too, will be an important part of the course, where we shall be able to learn from others and from each other. In addition, the Welsh Office has given a grant to enable us to monitor and evaluate the effects of the course, to record the successes and failures, and to gauge the strengths and limitations of different approaches.

None of us have any illusions about the size of the task or its difficulties. We do not claim that it is *the* way forward for dealing with prevention (even narrowly in an educational context). However, we hope and believe that it is *a* way forward for schools which has more chance of success than what has been tried in the past.

Bibliography

Gath, D. (1972) 'Child guidance and delinquency in a London borough.' *Psychological Medicine*, vol. 2, no. 2, pp. 185–91.

Peaker, G. F. (1967) 'The regression analyses of the national survey.' in Central Advisory Council for Education, *Children and Their Primary Schools* (Plowden Report) vol. 2 (London: HMSO).

Power, M. J., Benn, R. C. and Morris, J. N. (1972) 'Neighbourhood, school and juveniles before the courts', *British Journal of Criminology*, vol. 12, no. 2, pp. 111–32.

Reynolds, D. (1977) 'The delinquent school' in H. Hammersley and P. Woods (eds). *The Process of Schooling* (London: Routledge and Kegan Paul).

Rutter, M. (1973) 'Why are London children so disturbed?' *Proceedings of the Royal Society of Medicine*, vol. 66, no. 12, pp. 1221–5.

Wiseman, S. (1967) 'The Manchester survey', in Central Advisory Council for Education, *Children and Their Primary Schools* (Plowden Report) vol. 2 (London: HMSO).

9

Environments for Children

Colin Ward

Is the environment of the urban child better or worse than it used to be? From our own recollections or from the opening pages of innumerable autobiographies we may be likely to conclude that the contemporary child has a less happy habitat than that of his grandparents. Then we reflect that the distorting mirror of memory and the transforming power of nostalgia may be playing its usual tricks. For the social historians are at our elbows to remind us, as Laslett does, that

> Englishmen in 1901 had to face the disconcerting fact that destitution was still an outstanding feature of fully industrialised society, with a working class perpetually liable to social and material degradation. More than half of all the children of working men were in this dreadful condition, which meant 40 per cent of all the children in the country. These were the scrawny, dirty, hungry, ragged, verminous boys and girls who were to grow up into the working class of twentieth-century England. (1965)

The modern city child survives, while his predecessor a century ago frequently did not. But once we go beyond the giant steps to survival owed to sanitation, water supply, preventive medicine and social security, and attempt to look qualitatively at the lives the modern city offers to its children, doubts and worries emerge. We begin to think that there *is* a difference between the slums of hope and the slums of despair, and between being poor and being part of a culture of poverty.

The concept of a culture of poverty, like that of the cycle of deprivation, has given rise to passionate ideological argument. Lewis, the American anthropologist who invented the former phrase (1966), simply remarked that in Cuba, or in the squatter cities of Peru, Turkey, Athens, Hong Kong and Brazil, there are millions of poor people but little sign of a culture of poverty; and a related point, specifically to do with the environment of the urban child, emerged from the international survey directed for UNESCO by Lynch (1978). This was concerned with children of eleven to fourteen years in the city of Salta in Argentina; in the western suburbs of Melbourne, Australia; in Toluca, a provincial capital in Mexico and in Ecatepec, a largely dweller-built settlement on the northern fringe of Mexico City; in two contrasted neighbourhoods in Warsaw, and two similarly contrasted neighbourhoods of another Polish city, Cracow.

The UNESCO survey was probably the most ambitious attempt yet made to evaluate the relationship between children and the urban environment. The techniques used were those of 'cognitive mapping' (that is, the construction of 'mental maps' showing what aspects of the environment were important for them) and interviews. What emerges very clearly is that these older children's picture of the city and their part in it is conditioned by the esteem in which it is held by their elders. The Melbourne children for example, were certainly the most affluent in this international sample, they were 'tall, well dressed, almost mature, apparently full of vitality' but they see themselves as the bottom of society, and 'if these Australians have hopes for themselves or their children, it is to be somebody else, and to get away'. The Argentine children, on the other hand, are quite obviously conscious of being members of a community with 'features which make it amenable to change at their scale of possibility'. Only three of the interviewed children there thought they would leave the area in the future, while only three of the Melbourne children thought they would stay.

Alone in the UNESCO survey, the children of Ecatepec, the dweller-built settlement outside Mexico City, 'consistently named their school as a favourite place, and gave it a loving emphasis on their maps'. The suggestions they made to the interviewers 'reflect a genuine concern for their families, as well as their own future, and an empathy for fellow residents of the *colonia*'. They were the poorest children in the survey, and their environment seemed harsh, bleak and monotonous to the adult researchers. It is obvious from their report that they were puzzled by the unique affection for their school displayed by the children of Ecatepec in the maps, drawings and interviews. 'This must be a tribute to the public education in that place', they surmise. No such tribute would be offered by the children of an equivalently poor district in Detroit, Boston, London or Liverpool, though it might have been made there many years ago.

The parents of those Mexican children are poor rural migrants who made the great leap from rural hopelessness into the inner city slums of Mexico City. Once they had learned urban ways, they moved to a squatter settlement on the fringe of the city. In many such Latin American settlements the parents have built their own schools and hired their own teachers. For their children life is visibly improving, 'there is less dust now, houses that used to be shanties are fully constructed, one does not have to go outside the *colonia* for certain services . . .' The parents from Melbourne, with an infinitely higher standard of living, are conscious that they have not quite made it, and the stigmatisation of the district where they live communicates itself to the children. In this place where 'football clubs and schools have two-metre-high wire mesh fence around the periphery topped with barbed wire' and where parks are 'flat featureless tracts of haphazardly grassed unused land', the local authorities believe that 'space for organised team sport is what is most urgently needed, despite the lack of use of what already exists'.

Social space

It is hard, no doubt, for those who have devoted themselves to campaigning for physical space for the young in the city, a claim which is certainly self-justifying, to accustom themselves to the idea that, very early in life, another, just as urgent but more difficult to meet demand arises, for *social* space: the claim of the city's children to be a part of the city's life.

Kevin Lynch's own conclusion from his international survey was that the young people interviewed were victims of 'experiential starvation'. He found that distance is not the essential restriction on the movement of young adolescents away from their local areas. More important is the mixture of parental control, personal fear and a lack of knowledge of how to get about, as well as the availability and cost of public transport.

There are many other ways in which the contemporary urban environment is less usable, less comprehensible and less equipped with opportunities for growth into adulthood than the traditional city. Domination of the physical environment by the needs of the driver of the out-of-town motor vehicle is one example of this. Just try crossing a city like Birmingham on foot. The change in retail distribution from corner shop to supermarket, and the change in the pattern of housing from the street with front doors and back yards to the super-block are further examples of the way in which it is harder for the child to cope with his environment, let alone use it for his own purposes. It is not at all surprising that so many adolescents seem to be actively at war with their environment.

The boy or girl in the familiar background of poverty and deprivation is more and more isolated from the world of the successful and self- confident as time goes by. My wife once coined a profound aphorism in trying to define this isolation: 'As the threshold of competence rises, the pool of inadequacy increases.' In the modern city you have to be cleverer to cope. During the period of mushroom growth in the cities of Britain and America in the nineteenth century, the city child always had something to *do*, something to engage him in the experience of living. Usually of course he had too much to do: he had to consider himself lucky to work for intolerably long hours at some dreary labour which was beyond his strength and earned a pittance in the desperate struggle to get food for himself and his family. But he was not trapped in a situation where there was nothing economically rational for him to do and where his whole background and culture prevented him from benefiting from the expensively provided education machine, once beyond the tender atmosphere of the infant school.

The child who grows up in the poverty belt of the British or American city today is caught in a cage in which there is not even the illusion of freedom of action to change his situation, except of course in activities outside the law. Self-confidence and purposeful self-respect drain away from these children as they grow up because there is no way which makes sense to them, of becoming involved in their own city, except in a predatory way.

Isolation

Inner city teachers, even very experienced ones, are so accustomed to mobility, freedom of access to transport and social competence in getting around, that they are continually surprised that so many of the children they teach lead lives confined to a few streets. A survey of children under five in the Handsworth district of Birmingham found that just under half *never* went out to play. 'They have no access, either exclusive or shared, to play spaces at the front or back of the house, and their parents feared for their safety if they let them out' (Lozells Social Development Centre, 1975).

Describing an infants' school in Islington in North London, Cameron (1973) remarks that: 'The experience of many of these children during the first five years of their lives has been so limited that they come to school like so many blank pages. Near the school is a park and a busy Underground station, but many of the children have never been inside the park and some of them don't know what a tube train looks like. Asked what they did at the week-end, they usually say they just stayed at home.' Even when we assume that they *must* have been around by the time they reach thirteen or fourteen, we find that the world of such children is fantastically restricted. Teachers in a school on a housing estate in Bristol told me of the shock with which they learned that some of their teenage pupils had never been to the centre of the city. Teachers in the London borough of Brent told me of 13- and 14-year-olds who had never seen the Thames; teachers in the boroughs of Lambeth and Southwark, in schools a few hundred yards from the river told me of pupils who had never crossed it.

Innumerable studies of delinquent children in the world's cities stress their insecurity and isolation. Leissner (1969), with experience of both New York and Tel Aviv, remarks that 'street club workers were constantly aware of the feelings of isolation which pervaded the atmosphere'. In Chicago, Short and Strodtbeck (1965) noted that 'the range of gang boys' physical movements is severely restricted', not only for fear of other gangs, but also because of a 'more general lack of social assurance'. Patrick (1973) found the same 'social disability' in the Glasgow boys he observed. This lack of social assurance certainly does amount to a social disability for many city children. Some children steal, not because they have no access to the purchase money, but because they find it a less arduous transaction than the verbal encounter with the seller. They move like strangers through their own city.

A decade ago Hannam and his colleagues at the school of education of Bristol University set in motion an experiment in out-of-school education for what we then called the fourth year leavers in the city's secondary schools. Their report (1971) described how their student teachers were each given an afternoon a week with two or three young people in their final year at school who had rejected everything that school stood for. Often the student teachers, who were as shy and uncertain with these boys and girls as the latter were with them, found that they were introducing their charges, for the first time, to some of the excitements and delights of the city. Apart from the lessons implicit for the young teachers, the reluctant learners were gaining some slight insight into what the city held for them: aspects of urban life taken for granted by children from wealthier or more sophisticated families.

A more recent study from the same city by White and Brockington (1978), describes a logical extension to Hannam's work. The authors remark that 'children who have experienced ten years of a compulsory system that has channelled and labelled them as failures are not going to jump for joy at the prospect of an extended sentence'. Their Community Education Project was an attempt to provide, for a day or half a day a week, an alternative educational experience, based upon a club staffed by trainee teachers and social workers. One of the members of the club was Bill Lawson, and the authors explain his predicament thus:

On the day Bill spent at the project instead of travelling with his mates from school, he would come straight from home in the morning. Like all the others in the group Bill could claim a refund from school for the bus fare to club. Yet though Bill's house was over two miles from us he always walked. On wet days he would arrive completely soaked (since he possessed no waterproof coat) and often shivering with cold. In reply to our questioning why he hadn't caught the bus, Bill would merely retort that he liked walking. But towards the end of the Christmas term, as the weather grew colder and predictably wetter, Bill's arrival time became increasingly later and more sporadic. After two mornings in a row when he hadn't turned up (and we were assured by his mates that he wasn't ill or on holiday) one of us called in at his house after work. Bill was out, but his mum was at home. Had Bill given up coming because he was bored? 'Oh, no', reassured mum, 'he really enjoys going to the club, but when its wet he doesn't like walking all that way.' At the suggestion that Bill should catch the bus on rainy days, she smiled, 'It's no good; you see Bill walks because he doesn't know where to get off the bus at the other end and he won't ask the conductor.' Bill had lived in Bristol for all of his fifteen years. He had never seemed to us particularly introverted or shy. Indeed, if the reports from his mates were to be believed, he led a pretty wild social life with girls, pubs and discos. And yet he wouldn't ask a stranger the way to us.

The resourceful child

All our generalisations about the city child are about the poor or deprived child. The child from a better-off family, or simply from one more equipped with urban know-how, is far better able to exploit the wonderful potential that any city offers. He has learned how to use its facilities. Blessed is the child, rich or poor, with a hobby or a skill or an all-consuming passion, for he or she is motivated to utilise the city as a generator of happiness. There are plenty of juvenile passions of course which are generators of misery for other people, but it remains true that the child who is hooked on to some network built around a shared activity has found ways of making the city work for him.

An enormous range of possible experiences and activities are open to the city child, and as always the household which is accustomed to planning ahead and knows where to look things up, draws the maximum benefit from opportunities which are theoretically available to all the city's children. The leader of the Inner London Education Authority remarked to me sadly that 'What ever new facility we provide, we know in advance that it's the middle-class children who will draw the benefit.' Significantly it is the quality newspapers and not the popular ones which find it worthwhile to include features on holiday events and activities for children. In my own city those children who are endowed with what middle-class sociologists sneer at as 'middle-class values', are set upon an escalator of experiences and activities which they travel up, at the public expense, so that the gap continually widens in the degree of urban competence and control over their own destinies which they enjoy, compared with that of the children who never set foot on this escalator.

It would be presumptuous to claim that there is a 'solution' to the problem of the isolation and alienation of a significant proportion of the city's children, or that more spending on play spaces and on play groups, desirable as these are, provide the answer. It is quite certain that environmental education as a school activity is not a trendy fad but an essential compensatory device in trying to make the city observable and negotiable for its young. It is not a subject but an aspect of every kind of school subject, pressed into service to attempt to make children the masters rather than the victims of their environment. For example, Bob Pugh as head of physical education at Peckham Manor School adapted the sport of orienteering to the streets of south London, just to make his pupils at home in their own city.

So far as play facilities are concerned, one thing that observation of the behaviour of children makes clear, though it has only recently entered the enormous literature on children's play and has yet to affect environmental policies, is that children will play everywhere and with anything. A city that is really concerned with the needs of its young will make the whole environment accessible to them. Park and playground designers who usurp the creative capacities of the very children who are intended to use their work, by building play sculptures instead of providing the materials for children to make their own, or who have earnest conferences about the appropriate kind of fencing to use, should pause and think about the implications of Benjamin's remark (1974) that 'ideally there should be no fence; but when we reach that happy state we will have no need for adventure playgrounds'. For the fenced-off child ghetto sharpens the division between the worlds of adults and children, while Benjamin's whole case is that we should share the same world.

> The point is that the streets, the local service station, the housing estate stairway, indeed anything our urban community offers, is part of the natural habitat of the child. Our problem is not to design streets, housing, a petrol station or shops that can lend themselves to play, but to educate society to accept children on a participating basis.

This explains why it was possible for Dennis Woods of North Carolina State University to deliver a paper with the title 'Free the Children! Down with Playgrounds!'.

Mattern (1968) of Berlin underlines his point. 'One should be able to play everywhere, easily, loosely, and not be forced into a "playground" or "park". The failure of an urban environment can be measured in direct proportion to the number of "playgrounds"'. Such an approach of course could easily be seized upon as a

justification for *not* adapting the city parks to the needs of contemporary citizens, or for *not* creating pocket parks in vacant city
sites, and for not redressing the glaring imbalance in the areas of
public open space available to the inhabitants of rich and poor
districts of the city. But it underlines the urgency of Joe Benjamin's
remark about educating society to accept children on a participating
basis.

Exemplary enterprises

With this in mind, there are a few exemplary enterprises around that
provide glimpses of the ways in which children can be enfranchised as
citizens: given challenges and responsibilities and incentives to make
the city their own. One example is the Pioneer Railway in the Buda
Hills above Budapest. This is a well-known tourist attraction and the
reactions of Western visitors are interesting. Some see it as a carefully
contrived ideological device for inculcating in the young the virtues of
industrial discipline and for ensuring a supply of labour for the
railway system. Others are patronising and talk of the 'comic dignity'
of the 10- to 15-year-old boys and girls who run it. I don't think there
is anything comic about the children. The attraction for me is that the
Pioneer Railway is a way of putting an essential public service into the
hands of the young: of saying that they are citizens and can do
something for their fellow citizens.

My other exemplary enterprises are all in this country: the Great
George's Community Arts Project in Liverpool; and in London,
Centreprise – the bookshop, coffee shop, publishing house and
community resource in Hackney; Inter-Action's City Farm; and the
Notting Dale Urban Studies Centre. These activities are not there for
children in isolation: they aim to serve local people, young or old.
They are not intended as a device for getting the kids off the street or
as an antidote to vandalism. Nor are they there to entertain. They are
there to help citizens, young or old, to discover their own skills,
aptitudes and potentialities. They each have a focus. At the Great
George's Project, known locally as The Blackie (as it is housed in an
old blackened former church), it is the power of the expressive arts.
At Centreprise it is the power of the printed word. At the City Farm it
is the power of contact with the natural world of animals and plants.
And at the Notting Dale Urban Studies Centre, it is the power of
environmental knowledge, for children and adults alike, as a lever for

change. As well as its services for local and visiting school groups it is a resource for the tenants and residents of that battered and neglected district.

All these examples indicate that there are people around who have accepted the message that every step we make to take children out of the ghetto of childhood into a sharing of interests and activities with those of the adult world, is a step towards a more habitable environment for our fellow citizens, young or old.

Bibliography

Benjamin, J. (1974) *Grounds for Play* (London: Bedford Square Press).

Cameron, S. (1972) 'The list that praises and condemns', *The Teacher*, 28 April.

Hannam, C., Smyth, P. and Stephenson, N. (1971) *Young Teachers and Reluctant Learners* (Harmondsworth: Penguin).

Laslett, P. (1965) *The World We Have Lost* (London: Methuen).

Leissner, A. (1969) *Street Club Work in Tel Aviv and New York* (London: Longman).

Lewis, O. (1966) 'The culture of poverty', *Scientific American*, October.

Lozells Social Development Centre (1975) *Wednesday's Children: a Report on Under-Fives Provision in Handsworth* (Community Relations Commission).

Lynch, K. (1978) *Growing Up in Cities* (Cambridge, Mass.: MIT Press).

Mattern, H. (1968) Lecture at the Congress of the International Federation of Landscape Architects, June.

Patrick, J. (1973) *A Glasgow Gang Observed* (London: Eyre Methuen).

Short, J. F. and Strodtbeck, F. L. (1965) *Group Process and Gang Delinquency* (University of Chicago Press).

White, R. and Brockington, D. (1978) *In and Out of School* (London: Routledge and Kegan Paul).

Woods, D. 'Free the Children! Down With Playgrounds!' (unpublished paper).

10

Early Prevention and Intervention

Mia Kellmer Pringle

The past forty years have seen in this country what amounts to a revolution in children's health: they are taller, mature earlier and certain diseases have been virtually eliminated. Two points are worth noting: first, that a major change in relation to diet and health was made at a time when food supplies were threatened by blockade during the Second World War. Realising that starvation could imperil the future of a whole generation, special provision was made for expectant and nursing mothers, and for children; in addition, fair shares for all were ensured through rationing. The benefits of this courageous experiment are still evident today. Indeed, now it is obesity rather than undernourishment that has become a problem among children.

Secondly, spectacular progress was made once it was accepted that the treatment of established disease is not the most efficient way of ensuring general health. Instead, improved hygiene, operated through the unglamorous departments of public health, was one vital strand. Another was preventive medicine including vaccination, immunisation and inoculation, thanks to which certain diseases such as tuberculosis, scarlet fever, diphtheria and poliomyelitis have almost disappeared.

Now the major problems are handicap; accidents at home and on the roads; neglect, rejection and abuse of children; and the effects on them of the break-up of marriages. It is in these areas that effective methods of prevention, and if need be intervention, should be developed and applied. Not only is the 'prevention better than cure' maxim obviously true in these as in any other aspects of child health and development; but it is also less costly in terms of human happiness, both children's and adults'. Yet we have been slower to act than have some other West European countries. There is now a sufficient understanding of some of the broad preventive measures needed to achieve a significant reduction; and such measures must start early.

How early is 'early'?

Evidence is now accumulating to show how early 'early' is. Even before birth the infant is a responsive and responding creature. During the latter part of pregnancy the foetus can see and hear: a soft red light or certain kinds of sound cause it slowly to turn, while a bright light and certain noises can startle the unborn child. During this same period in pregnancy, some foetuses seem to signal their personalities to the mother, some being quiet and others active. Then shortly after birth, the baby likes to watch the human face and soon comes to recognise and prefer that of his mother; similarly, he will turn his head towards her voice.

Bonding

Burton L. White of Harvard is reported to have said: 'God or someone has built into the human infant a collection of attributes that guarantee attractiveness.' Perhaps this assists the mechanism of 'bonding' between mother and infant which also starts very early. Both are vital to the baby's existence, since he has to be 'demanding' in the sense that without food, warmth and loving care, he cannot survive. A number of recent American studies set out to promote this early mother–infant tie, by encouraging body contact, nursing and care straight after delivery and in the following few days. This clearly benefited both: the mothers were more involved with their babies, more soothing, fondled them more and were more reluctant to leave them in the care of others; these differences continued to be observed also a year later.

Two years later, there were still differences, the mothers who had had early and more intensive contact with their infants, speaking with them more and being more relaxed in their handling. The effect on the children was still observable at the age of five years: compared with the control group, where mothers and babies had experienced the normal hospital routine, the children were significantly better in both language and intellectual development (Hirsh and Levin, 1978).

Studies of mothers and newborns in other cultures obtained similar results. Some Swedish studies, for example, found that mothers showed more affection to their babies when they had been allowed to hold them naked against their own bodies; while the infants smiled more and cried less in subsequent months. The father, too, is reported to remain closer to the child if he attends the birth, so that he both sees and holds the newborn in the first few hours. This has led to the hypothesis that major preventive mental health measures could be launched at relatively modest cost in the perinatal period. The apparent value of mother–infant contact in the first minutes and hours following birth serves to underline the critical importance of the maternal role. It also demonstrates how complex and sensitive even the newborn is, and that the social and emotional interaction between infant and care-givers is an individual and intricate process.

Earliest interaction

Another example shows how early individual differences can be observed as well as the early interaction between nature and nurture. Stable individual differences have been found in motor activity of newborns both in hospital and at home. The mothers of the more active infants were more demonstrative towards their babies and appeared to form a stronger and earlier attachment to them. Here is the beginning of an egg-and-chicken question: a more active baby probably calls out stronger maternal feelings and a more 'motherly' mother is likely to encourage a baby to be more active and responsive.

Thus, growing understanding of the earliest stages of human development indicates how early 'early' is, and the significance of even the intrauterine environment and the first few days and weeks of life for the infant's future development. It is then that the mother and child begin to interact and influence one another. Full-time mothering is unique in the sense that the mother has the time, and hence the patience, to develop sensitivity to her baby. This enables her to recognise and adapt to its very special, individual needs (Brazelton, 1969; Rossi, 1977).

Such maternal involvement and participation in the child's progress is the quality now recognised as being of crucial importance to optimal development. A mother who can give only hurried and preoccupied attention is unlikely to be able to develop this awareness.

Also because infants have a short memory span, she will not very readily provide a consistent, continuing 'model'. Thus it is the quality, dependability and consistency of parental – usually maternal – care and the close involvement in the child's earliest learning, that offer the best chance for optimal physical, emotional and intellectual development.

Disadvantages which impede such optimal development not only begin long before children are born but are more often than not, multiple, cumulative, continuing and mutually reinforcing. For example, prematurity, low birth weight and perinatal complications are related to the mother's reproductive efficiency; this depends upon her age, nutrition, stature, the number of children she already has, whether or not she smokes, and so on. All these are likely to be less favourable for women in the lowest socio-economic group. Moreover, some of these disadvantages influencing a baby's chances can be traced back even further – to the mother's own childhood: her stature will have been affected by the adequacy of her own nutrition when young, just as her capacity to provide loving care for her baby will largely depend on the quality of mothering she herself received. Hence prevention – and where need be intervention – must start long before a baby's birth and continue throughout its childhood (Pilling and Pringle, 1978).

The size of the problem

Handicap

The exact number of handicapped children in the country is not known but it is estimated that one child in seven suffers from some disability, whether physical, emotional, intellectual or educational; this estimate includes the whole range, from mild and moderate to severe impairment. In the last mentioned group alone, there are thought to be some 33 000 children (DES, 1978).

How well a handicapped child is able to cope with life, whether or not he can manage to hold his own in an ordinary school or needs special provision of one kind or another, and how he makes out in the long run, do not – as might be expected – depend primarily on the nature, severity or onset of his condition. It is the attitudes of his parents first and foremost, then those of his peers and teachers and of society at large, that appear to have an over-riding effect: they determine how he will feel about himself and his handicap. This is illustrated by the vivid biographies of those who have triumphed over severe disabilities and is confirmed by many studies (Brown, 1954; Carlson, 1952; Pilling, 1973; Pringle, 1964a, 1964b; Pringle and Fiddes, 1970). Clearly this has implications both for prevention and intervention.

Accidents

The latest available figures for accidental deaths among children aged 0–15 years is about 1800, of which some 700 occurred on the roads. In fact, accidents are now the largest single cause of death for this age group. The figure for non-fatal accidents is, of course very much higher; for example, accidental poisoning alone accounted for about 16 000 hospital admissions in the same year (Jackson, 1977). Most probably an even greater number of accidents to children do not get reported and thus do not find their way into the statistics. What is beyond doubt is that they account for an enormous amount of anxiety, distress and pain; and that a high proportion are preventable.

Abuse

How many children are neglected, rejected and seriously abused is even more a matter of guesswork. The most reliable estimates indicate that annually about 8000 suffer 'non-accidental injuries' – the euphemism now officially used for 'battering' in the case of children; significantly it is not used for assaulted wives because, being adults, they would protest against such belittling circumlocution which conceals the reality of their suffering. Of these, about 1600 receive such serious injuries at the hands of their parents that permanent brain damage, paralysis, blindness or mental handicap may result. How many are actually killed remains a matter of dispute, estimates ranging from one hundred a year to three or four times this figure (Kempe and Kempe, 1978; Franklin, 1978; Pringle, 1978).

   Until there is compulsory notification of all non-accidental injuries the true incidence will not be known. Even then, the whole truth may not come to light for a number of reasons. Among them is the fact that parents (and others) do not always kill children in easily ascertainable or dramatic ways which can be identified by pathologists. Also some of the causes of death in the official statistics may not be as innocent as their designation implies.

Examples are suffocation by pressing a hand or pillow against the baby's face; or death from pneumonia or bronchitis in infants who have 'failed to thrive' because of physical or emotional neglect or both. In addition, actual battering is only the visible tip of the iceberg. Hundreds if not thousands of children suffer daily emotional rejection and abuse.

The break-up of families

Again exact figures are not easily obtainable. It looks as if as many as 15 per cent of children may during some period of their childhood not be cared for by both their natural parents. They may then live in a one-parent family or they may have started life in such a family. This may turn into a two-parent family, one being a step-parent or cohabitee. Also at any one time some 100 000 children are entirely separated from their family, living in a residential setting or in a substitute home (Ferri, 1976; Prosser, 1976).

Approaches to prevention and intervention

The underlying principles should be to accord priority to early prevention rather than to crisis intervention, as at present; parents, or those who stand *in loco parentis*, should be accepted as full partners since they not only know the child, with his strengths and weaknesses, better than anyone else but they always share and often carry the major part of the responsibility for the child's care, treatment and rehabilitation. A further principle should be that intervention must promote the best interests of the child rather than merely remove him/her from harmful experiences.

The aims of professionals and the services they provide should be to complement and supplement the care and education which the vast majority of loving and concerned parents provide for their children. Only when these are deficient in some respects, are intervention and the provision of compensatory services required. When parental care is damaging to the child's well-being or entirely lacking, then substitute care has to be provided; this must, however, not only be better in the sense of being more conducive to optimal development, but also therapeutic in the sense of healing the damage done, be this emotional, social, intellectual or physical.

There are four major preventive approaches which would go a long way to reduce the incidence of handicap, accidents, abuse and family break-up. These are preparation and support for parenthood; genetic counselling and antenatal care; accident prevention; and regular developmental check-ups, at least for pre-school children.

Preparation and support for parenthood

At present, secondary schools include in the curriculum what may appear to many pupils a hotchpotch of unconnected subjects, such as sex education, home economics, health education, civic or political education, and social education. While all of them have a bearing on human development and on children's future adult roles, this fragmentation into separate subjects all too often fails to provide a coherent and meaningful framework.

Such a framework could be given by including instead two new areas of knowledge in the curriculum of all secondary schools for both boys and girls and for pupils of all levels of ability: first, an understanding of human psychology; and secondly, preparation for parenthood. Not only would they offer a unifying theme but the focus and starting point would be the adolescents themselves. Since at this stage of development personal relationships, feelings and doubts are a normal preoccupation of young people, their interest and involvement would readily be enlisted.

A knowledge of human psychology would include the dynamics of behaviour, the ways in which people interact and react at a great variety of levels, the role of values and the roots of prejudice. The opportunity to acquire a fairly sophisticated understanding of the sequential nature of human development, of the various stages of physical and mental growth, of motivation and of the wide variations in behaviour, including deviancy, would complement and supplement what children will have learnt already. Such learning will have taken place in their own families and in their relationships with contemporaries as well as having come about through reading stories and through the media. However, teachers can present such knowledge in a more systematic, more generalised and less personal way. To learn about the reasons why we feel and respond as we do, and about the complexity and variety of relationships, is surely a basic prerequisite for adult maturity and for an understanding of one's self? Without it, social, political and sex education lack a secure base.

Preparation for parenthood is logically based on such a broad background of human psychology. After all, the vast majority of young people will themselves become parents and understanding children is greatly helped by an understanding both of oneself and of the normal stages of development. Some people may claim that preparation for parenthood is already undertaken in schools up and down the country, either in courses on home economics, health education or citizenship (now renamed 'political education'). However, the first mentioned concentrates primarily on household management, home buying, budgeting, hygiene and nutrition; health education usually encompasses diet, exercise, smoking, drinking, drugs and other health hazards; and political education is mainly concerned with giving young people knowledge of our democratic institutions, both at local and national levels, the law, race relations, the processes of decision-making and the citizen's rights, in some cases linking the subject with voluntary service in the community.

Providing an effective programme An effective programme of preparation for parenthood must have a broad base. An understanding of human psychology and child development is the essential foundation. Sex education, family planning, home economics and political education as well as first-hand practical experience of babies and young children would form an integral part of the programme.

Few schools do as yet provide such a broadly-based scheme but the vast majority have for some time been offering their pupils sex education. With hindsight, this may have done more harm than good since an appropriate perspective on this topic can only be achieved within the context of affectionate, mutually responsible relationships between the sexes rather than within the narrower biological setting of reproductive processes, child-birth, contraception and venereal diseases. Significantly enough, the need for a wider programme is well appreciated by young people themselves.

That this is so was clearly shown by the results of a study which revealed that the physical aspects of human reproduction were taught in most schools (90 per cent). Yet only a minority (some 30 per cent) of school leavers have had sufficient opportunity to learn about child development and the practical problems of family life. Indeed, the majority felt the need to know more about these areas of adult responsibility (Fogelman, 1976). Surely, it is irresponsible to provide sex education except within the context of the caring human relationships involved. But this was done in far fewer schools.

Developing programmes of preparation for parenthood in all our schools would be a first step towards translating into practice the belief that children are society's seedcorn for the future. Concern with improving the quality of life of everyone must start with the young of today. To begin with, they should be helped to achieve a more realistic understanding of parenthood long before they decide whether or not to become parents. This must be based on a truly objective appreciation of its demands, constraints, satisfactions and challenges.

Paradoxically, home-making and parenting, especially mother-hood, are simultaneously both under- and overvalued. On the one hand, the housewife with young children, whose working hours are, on average, twice as long as that of the 35-hour-a-week worker, is described and treated as not being gainfully employed. The father's role and essential involvement are rarely mentioned. On the other hand, an over-romanticised picture of motherhood prevails in our society and is reinforced by the media.

Instead, a more truthful, even daunting, awareness needs to be created of the arduous demands which child-rearing makes not only on the emotions, energy, time, but also on financial resources. These are most acutely felt when the first baby comes along. The inevitable constraints on personal independence, freedom of movement and indeed one's whole way of life, require to be spelt out. Babies should be presented as they are, warts and all, rather than as heart-warmingly attractive, invariably sunny tempered with a dimply, angelic smile.

For this realistic portrayal to be believed, it must be seen to be true – hence the importance of first-hand experience with babies and young children. There are many different ways in which this could be provided. What is vital is that it should be viewed in the same way as laboratory work in chemistry or physics – work to be done regularly for a considerable period of time. In this way, the physical care required by babies and toddlers will also come to be appreciated more realistically than by using dolls as models.

Family planning–parental age and family size Preparation for parenthood is a natural vehicle for enabling boys and girls to learn about the relationship between the sexes and how these inevitably change when children come along, as well as for setting sex education and family planning into an appropriate context. The reasons why very young couples more often have serious difficulties in undertaking parenthood arise from considering the needs of children. Very young parents are themselves not yet fully mature emotionally or socially and therefore are less able to provide the emotional support so vital for a child's optimal development. Financial and housing difficulties are likely additional problems for those at the beginning of their working life. The cumulative effects and inter-relationships of all these factors probably account for the fact that the rate of marriage breakdown is highest among such couples.

Thus, postponing parenthood until both partners are fully mature is in the best interest not only of their own long-term relationship but also of their future child. Similarly, family planning can be linked with the concept that responsible parenthood means having only as many children as a couple can emotionally tolerate and financially afford. This fact is demonstrated by the evidence showing that children from large families are at a considerable disadvantage physically, educationally and in terms of social adjustment.

Family size begins to exert an unfavourable influence right from birth onwards, high perinatal mortality being associated with high parity. Also children with many siblings are shorter than those with few and the arrival of each additional child appears to act subsequently as a check to the growth of all preceding, that is, older children; so the first-born does not reach the height of an only child when there are younger children. Nor is it solely a question of low income and thus a lower standard of living: these effects of family size upon development operate irrespective of social class. When parental time, attention and maybe also patience, have to be shared, then less is available for each child. Thus large families put a strain on both financial and psychological resources.

Helping young people to achieve a more realistic understanding of parenthood may lead some couples to question whether they are really willing to devote the necessary time, energy and money to caring for children. For the majority, it will remain the most creative and responsible task available to them. In the foreseeable future, many young people will continue to have to work at dull, repetitive jobs and indeed some will not be able to find any employment at all. Until and unless this situation changes, parenthood will provide the major source of personal fulfilment and of creativity for many of them.

Promoting and supporting good parenting Preparation for parent-hood in one sense starts at birth since a child learns about it through his own experience of family life. However, those deprived of adequate parental care have little chance of becoming in turn responsible parents themselves. In any case, it might raise both the status and the level of parenting if the total population were to receive some preparation for the task. The earliest, and in a sense best, opportunity to achieve this occurs with school children because they are in effect a captive audience.

To be fully effective, subsequent opportunities must continue to be available for young people, including couples expecting their first child, to prepare themselves for parenthood. Youth organisations, centres for further and adult education, advice and counselling services for young people as well as pregnancy advisory, maternity and marriage guidance services, all have a part to play in this task (Pugh, 1980). If such opportunities became freely and readily available, then the parental life-style may come to be chosen more deliberately in the fuller realisation of its responsibilities and satisfactions.

Presenting a much enhanced image of home-making and child-rearing should become part of this realisation. Otherwise the dangerous trend towards making children pawns in the quest for economic prosperity and in the battle for women's liberation will continue. The risks of allowing this to happen are great – both in terms of the children's happiness and of society's future.

Society, and hence government, should acknowledge the import-ance of parental care by four supportive measures. First, by really adequate index-linked child benefit so that no woman (or man for that matter) who wishes to devote herself full-time to the care of her pre-school children needs to seek employment outside the home for financial reasons. Other countries such as Sweden, France and Hungary already operate such systems of allowances linked to a proportion of average earnings. Also pension rights should be safeguarded so that the breaks in continuity of work do not curtail long-term benefits.

Secondly, for pre-school children who require substitute day care, high quality, comprehensively conceived day facilities should be provided which combine both care and education. For the under-threes these facilities should be based on substitute families, and given that the first measure was to be translated into reality, would be mainly designed for a small minority, such as infants of mentally or physically handicapped or sick mothers, one-parent families, and those who are rejected or abused.

For the over-threes, comprehensive pre-school centres would provide care combined with educational facilities. The majority would be able to go to nursery schools or playgroups if their mothers wished them to do so, the aim of which would be to complement and supplement parental care.

Thirdly, once children go to school, refresher courses and re-training facilities should be provided for mothers who wish to return to work; also suitable employment conditions will need to be introduced including flexible working hours to fit in with the relatively short school day and the long holidays. The years devoted by a mother to child-rearing should be fully taken into account for incremental and promotion purposes since for the vast majority of jobs the experience and skills gained are relevant and of value to demands and expectations of the world of work. In that way, parents would not be penalised for the time given to child-rearing.

Fourthly, even if the three measures just outlined were to be adopted, the inevitable stresses and strains of family life and child-rearing will threaten to break up some marriages. To prevent this from happening unnecessarily, support services in times of crisis will need to be available more readily than is the case at present.

Chief among them are marriage guidance, marital counselling, marital and family therapy, and child guidance. For these services to be expanded to meet existing need would require substantially increased government support. It would also mean giving much greater priority to families – especially those with young children – in terms of fiscal, housing, income maintenance, job training and health policies, so as to reduce social and economic pressures on couples during the most demanding years of child-rearing.

When Parliament in 1969 passed a Bill to make divorce easier and quicker than it had been hitherto, the aims of the reformers were, in the words of one of them (Abse, 1979), 'to have a divorce law that helped to buttress rather than undermine the stability of marriage . . . Parliament hoped that the in-built reconciliation procedures elaborated within the Divorce Reform Act would direct warring parties to marital guidance agencies and probation officers so that no saveable marriage would end. Unhappily, reconciliation provisions within the Act are proving to be an almost total failure.'

This failure could be rectified if a recent government-sponsored report were to be implemented (Home Office, 1979). Here, too, prevention is better than cure, and the toll of broken marriages would also be reduced if marriage and child-bearing were not embarked upon until the twenties, as has been argued earlier.

Genetic counselling and antenatal care　As control of other causes of perinatal and infant death has improved, genetic disorders have become more important; they now account for an increasing proportion of morbidity and mortality. About one in four infant deaths and about one in twenty admissions of children to hospital are due to disorders which are largely or even entirely genetic in causation. Also they can cause handicap both in early and in later life (DHSS, 1977; Emery, 1977).

Genetic counselling for parents at risk of having an affected child could prevent at least a proportion of such disorders. Therefore if a couple have reason for anxiety or if they already have an affected child, it should be readily available to them. This would be facilitated by a close link between family planning and antenatal care services on the one hand, and genetic counselling facilities on the other.

The counsellor's task would be to discuss with prospective parents the nature of a genetic disorder, its likely severity, and whether or not an effective treatment exists, as well as the probability of recurrence. The couple would then be able to assess the risk of having a handicapped child and, if they decide to go ahead with a pregnancy, to become aware of possible treatments, likely educational needs and long-term prospects. In this way the counsellor would assist them in choosing the course of action which seems most appropriate in the light not only of genetic but social, psychological, economic and other relevant factors, all of which will have a bearing on their ability to cope with a handicapped child.

Early and regular antenatal care is another vital preventive measure. Designed to anticipate the likely needs of both the pregnant woman and the developing foetus, it aims to ensure the safe delivery of a healthy baby. On the basis of the expectant mother's present state of health and her medical, obstetric and family history, those who are at special risk can be detected early and, if need be, given special care.

Also, the sooner she obtains her certificate of expected confinement, the sooner she can avail herself of free milk, vitamins and prescriptions, as well as free dental treatment.

Despite the evident advisability of seeking early antenatal care, by no means all pregnant women do so. Indeed, according to a recent report (DHSS, 1977) 'a worryingly large number still fail to keep appointments or do not attend until much later and some are still unknown to the health service until they go into labour. Studies have shown that the perinatal death rate is nearly five times higher in the children of mothers who are late in booking (making arrangements for care in pregnancy) than in those who are early.' Worse still, research shows that those women whose need for antenatal care is greatest tend to seek it either very late or never (Crellin, Pringle and West, 1971; DHSS, 1976 and 1977; Vowles *el al.*, 1975).

To encourage pregnant women to make earlier and regular use of antenatal services, some countries have introduced incentive payments. For example, in France various maternity benefits are paid on proof of having visited a clinic as well as for undergoing specific medical tests (Wynn and Wynn, 1972–3, 1977). Such visits can also be used for persuading expectant mothers not to smoke cigarettes, which would do more to reduce infant mortality in the United Kingdom than any other single measure (Butler *et al.*, 1972).

Accident prevention

Technological developments have introduced new and increased hazards into children's environments. Just to mention three: in the home, many labour-saving devices and other domestic equipment present risks to them; so do toxic chemical preparations and medicines; and the roads have become more dangerous as the number of car users has grown. Yet insufficient guidance is given to parents to develop a greater understanding of both the physical and psychological factors which make children peculiarly liable to suffer accidents.

Developmental immaturity is one such factor. For example, normal, healthy curiosity coupled with inevitably limited intellectual understanding, inexperience and a short memory span mean that safe storage out of a young child's reach is essential to prevent his drinking or swallowing harmful substances. Explanations and threats are as inappropriate as punishment, since only time will bring about the necessary level of maturation and awareness. Another example relates to traffic. Children under the age of twelve years have great difficulty in localising sounds or judging the speed of moving objects – aspects which are vital to coping with crossing roads. Their capacity to do so is greatly overestimated by mothers; a survey showed that over half of them thought it was safe to let their 5-year-old cross a main road by himself (Sadler, 1972). Another study found that as many as 26 per cent of mothers considered their 2-year-olds able to cross the road outside their homes by themselves (DOE, 1973).

Making the environment much more 'child proof' and providing satisfactory supervision appropriate to the child's age and level of understanding, are essential if a significant reduction of accidents is to be brought about. Improving parental understanding and expectations of children's capacities and capabilities on the one hand, and promoting their acceptance of safety and precautionary measures on the other hand, is only one aspect of what is required. Parents also need to press local and central government as well as designers and manufacturers to give much higher priority to accident prevention. The design of roads and playgrounds; of homes and schools; of cars and bicycles; of household gadgets and medicine containers; these are only a few examples of areas where child deaths and injuries could be substantially reduced by paying greater attention to the well-being and needs of children.

There is perhaps too ready an acceptance of what seems to be the inevitability of accidents – the word itself induces a fatalistic resistance to the possibility of prevention. 'The word "accident" unfortunately and wrongly implies an unpredictable and therefore unpreventable event' (Jackson, 1977). In outlining the stages of an accident prevention programme, the same author emphasises the importance of the developmental and psychosocial factors in childhood accidents. The first need is to collect satisfactory data and to analyse them in terms of the types and results of the accidents, the ages and personalities of the families and other people involved, as well as the overall circumstances; next, the principal 'avoidable factors' in the chain of events culminating in the accident have to be identified so that these can be altered, that is, a misleading road sign or the design of a spin dryer; then comes what is perhaps the most difficult stage, namely altering people's behaviour in accepting safety features and changing their perceptions of children's understanding of hazards and risks; finally, the cost-effectiveness and cost benefits of making the environment safer for children need to be worked out.

What has been concluded about children's safety in traffic seems to apply to all accidents to them: 'In the end, adults are always to blame for traffic accidents involving children. Working with traffic problems makes one aware of the fact that not only do adults overestimate children's limited ability with traffic but that adults themselves have very negative attitudes towards traffic, e.g. crossing the street against a red pedestrian light. This attitude is readily copied by children' (Sandels, 1975). Of course, the temptation to cross against a red light would be much reduced if the phasing of pedestrian crossing lights was altered to assist pedestrians instead of primarily traffic circulation. All adults will have to adopt a more positive attitude to accident prevention; only then will they develop a more realistic appreciation of how to reduce the risks of accidents to children.

Child abuse and corporal punishment

If attitudes towards the physical punishment of children are to be changed, then it may well be most effective if a start is made with today's young people. The topic would quite naturally arise within the context of a broadly based programme of preparation for parenthood. A starting point could be the intriguing paradox that as a society we disapprove of violence against the person and express particular disapproval of violent behaviour by children and young people. Yet physical chastisement – surely a form of violence – is widely practised against the young, both by their parents and those standing *in loco parentis* as a means of 'disciplining' them.

Indeed so much is it a part of child-rearing, that even the majority of young children are regularly hit by their parents; as many as 62 per cent apparently smack their one year olds and 93 per cent their four year olds, 17 per cent of whom were smacked at least once a day (Newson, 1970). Parents are more likely to use a hand only and to use corporal punishment more for younger children. In contrast, teachers are most likely to use an instrument, such as the cane or tawse, and it is most frequently employed against secondary school pupils (Fogelman, 1976); however, it is a permitted form of discipline even for five-year-old infants and is also meted out to children who are physically or mentally handicapped.

The belief in the usefulness of corporal punishment is curious when there is no evidence to support it. On the contrary, several studies have shown that children are better behaved in schools where physical chastisement is not used (Rutter *et al.*, 1979); and the fact that all too often the same pupils are repeatedly punished in this way clearly demonstrates its ineffectiveness in changing behaviour.

Those experienced in training dogs and other animals know that the infliction of pain is not a good method for bringing about desired behaviour – why then do we continue to believe it to be so in relation to the human young? Also our society no longer believes in the ennobling effects of pain – instead people consume a vast array of medicines and drugs to escape discomfort and alleviate pain; why then do we continue to cling to the belief that deliberately inflicted pain on the young is educative and morally reforming?

For some years now, all forms of physical punishments have been abolished by law in the armed forces, in prisons, borstals and detention centres. So is it not illogical – in the face of all this evidence – as well as quite unjust, to continue to inflict corporal punishment on children? Is it not hypocritical to condemn their aggressive behaviour when we practise it on them as a matter of course; and disingenuous when we profess to set children a good example of how to behave by the way we ourselves do? Physical chastisement may even be counterproductive since it not only arouses aggression but equally important teaches the child an unintended but none the less obvious lesson: that 'might is right' and hence if you are bigger you can intimidate and hit those weaker than yourself.

A climate of opinion in which corporal punishment of children is accepted and approved, is likely to reduce the threshold at which some parents are prepared to use grave physical violence against even quite young babies. They would see it merely as a matter of degree rather than as offending against the basic principle that it is morally wrong to assault young, helpless and dependent human beings. Maybe child abuse will only be eradicated when we determine that the time has come to condemn and abstain from all physical punishment of children in the same way as we have for many years now abolished its use against adults.

All European countries – except Eire and the United Kingdom – have outlawed the use of corporal punishment in schools. One country, Sweden, has now shown the way by no longer allowing parents to use it either. 'It is a natural historical development. We have already outlawed the striking of wives and servants. Opinion polls show it is time to make it illegal to hit children at home . . . Enforcing the law that a child may not be subjected to physical punishment or other offensive treatment will, of course, be impossible. It is rather for society to make clear to parents that it does not agree with the physical punishment of children' (booklet published by the Swedish Department of Justice 1979, setting out guidelines for parents; at present available in Swedish only).

What effective methods of discipline are there then, if it is accepted that their aim must be to instil self-discipline and self-control? Basically, it is the parents' own standards, values and beliefs which provide the foundation for the child's eventual conduct; they provide not only the first but also the most intimately observed models whose behaviour and attitudes in turn shape the child's.

The more discipline is based on reasoning and discussion, the more readily understanding develops of parental standards and expectations. The latter need to be appropriate to the child's age and understanding while punishments should be logically related to the 'offence'; thus they would range from having to forego a treat or privilege to having to make restitution, and from being scolded to being temporarily isolated because of antisocial behaviour. In this way the child comes to feel shame and guilt when s/he does something s/he knows his or her parents would disapprove of; and so s/he eventually develops a 'conscience' through anticipating likely parental (and then increasingly other people's) expectations and reactions.

Developmental checks

Here again, it is those children most in need of regular developmental checks who are least likely to get them. 'The greatest problem for children in our present society is the law of inverse care, namely that the better-off families, whose need is generally least, make the optimal use of the services provided, while poorer families whose need is commonly greatest make the least use of available resources' (Vowles *et al.*, 1975).

The findings from the Bureau's National Child Development Study as well as recent DHSS figures fully confirm that this is the case in relation to the uptake of all free services. For example, less than half of the country's under-fives attend health centres; one child in three is now not being taken for either polio or measles vaccinations.

A large-scale French project, started in 1969, revealed the extent of unrecognised handicap in early childhood. At ten months and at two years, only one-third of the infants received a completely clean bill of health, while 10 per cent were considered to require urgent treatment if their future was not to be prejudiced. In most cases the parents had been unaware that anything was amiss. French cost-benefit studies also show that the earlier the intervention and treatment, the lower the cost and the greater the benefits (A. Wynn, 1976; M. Wynn, 1976).

For prevention to be successful, regular developmental checks are essential. The youngest age group is the most vulnerable; hence theirs is the greatest need for checks. Only treatment given in good time can prevent some handicaps. For example, the amelioration of conditions such as phenylketonuria, which causes severe mental handicap and deafness, is most likely to be effective if treatment is begun during the first few months of life. Also very young children, who are ill-treated are particularly vulnerable, being unable to appeal for help or even to run away from home – always a serious danger signal in a small child.

Developmental checks must be multidisciplinary, covering all areas of growth: physical and sensory development; adaptive development; communication; self-help; emotional and social development, which includes relationships with both adults and other children.

Physical checks   These would include height, weight, posture, vision, hearing as well as the growth and control of body movements.

Adaptive development   This can be seen in the co-ordination of sight with fine movements such as the ability to hold a pencil, opening a door, catching a ball with both hands and using a bat to hit a ball.

Communication   This is concerned with the development of speech and the understanding of language – from saying one clear word to trying to sing a nursery rhyme, talking in short phrases of three words or more, describing what is happening in a picture rather than just naming the object.

Self-help   This relates to the growing child's desire and ability to do more and more for himself – helping to hold a cup or bottle or feeding himself with a spoon, remaining usually dry through the night or managing to dress without supervision.

Emotional and social development These would be concerned with the way the baby responds to his mother and then to other adults and children – smiling at the person who feeds him, demonstrating affection by kissing or hugging, showing an interest in other children, playing co-operatively with them.

The frequency of developmental checks could decrease as the child gets older. For example, there might be four during the first twelve months, two a year during the second and third year and then annual checks for three- to five-year-olds. There are even more in Sweden in the first year (five) and in Finland (ten); both countries achieve almost complete coverage of the child population.

Of course, we do have developmental checks in Britain, and both health visitors and paediatricians play an important role in early preventive health care. But nothing like 100 per cent coverage is achieved during the first five years of childhood.

Achieving complete coverage

Could complete coverage be achieved in the United Kingdom? Clearly publicity about the value of such checks – via the press, women's magazines, television and radio – could play an important part; but it will not of itself be sufficient. Better results are likely to be obtained by the use of cash incentives, such as the £30 payments for the pregnancy examination and for the first antenatal check paid in Finland.

In France the incentive process has been taken further. For an early antenatal examination and further checks during pregnancy about £156 is paid to the mother. A full paediatric examination of the child at eight days old entitles the mother to a further £100 while two further checks, at nine months and two years, bring £50 each. These payments have achieved almost complete coverage of all mothers-to-be and then their young children. In total they come to about £250 million a year and are regarded as cost-effective, because this amount is more than recouped by reductions in social security payments for sickness and handicap.

So despite the considerable total involved, prevention is still proving cheaper than cure. When restraints on public expenditure can be relaxed would it not be worthwhile introducing a similar system here? Meanwhile the only practical immediate measure would be to make the payments of child benefit dependent on the infant being given a series of developmental checks.

Parental rights and responsibilities

Critics may say that to operate financial incentives or sanctions backed, as a last resort, by law enforcement is a restriction or infringement on the liberty of the individual. But parents are obliged to send their children to school for eleven years or to provide suitable education by other means; no doubt this was also once seen as an infringement of their liberties.

Others may fear that children of poor parents may be penalised if they are unable or unwilling to take them for regular checks. But these could take place in their own homes or in day-care facilities in which many of the most disadvantaged under-fives are placed. Also, in cases of need, transport could be provided or travelling expenses reimbursed. The success of domiciliary family planning services in Aberdeen has shown the cost effectiveness of this approach.

In the case of school attendance, parents who wish to provide alternative schooling must convince a court of law that their children are receiving a suitable and adequate education. Similarly, parents not wishing to attend the nationwide developmental checks would have to demonstrate that they provided a nurturing home background for the child, which ensured adequate physical and emotional care. If the court was satisfied that the child's interests were being safeguarded, then the child benefit would be paid.

The French system also contains a residual power to withdraw family allowances if parents neglect to take a child for checks. So far, it has not proved necessary for these powers to be exercised. However, they make it possible to trace parents who have moved house, which ensures that reminder notices will actually reach them.

No doubt some will wish to represent this suggested sanction as being unwarranted state intrusion into the privacy of family life. Critics will also argue that it is unnecessary to enforce developmental checks for all children when only a minority are likely to be either handicapped, rejected or abused. However, to judge by the French experience, this minority is very sizeable: at least one in three children.

Is there not a parallel with the preventive measures now in force because of hijacking? Events over recent years have prepared air travellers to submit to a thorough search of luggage as well as their own persons, even though it involves greater inconvenience, more time and, of course, additional costs. In order to protect the tiny minority who might be subjected to hijacking, the vast majority of travellers willingly accept these restrictions of their 'freedom'. Surely there is an equally strong, if not a stronger case, for protecting the young? Children are the most dependent, and at the same time, the most helpless and vulnerable members of society. In fact, the vast majority of parents are likely to welcome regular developmental checks since these will ensure that their child's needs are discovered as early as possible, so that special help can be made available; and those whose children do not require such help will be reassured about the normality of their progress.

Parental freedom and privacy have to be balanced against another major right which should equally concern society: a child's elementary right to loving care and protection, both of his physical and mental health. After all, the state gives an allowance to parents in order to encourage good child care. Is it not common sense and good housekeeping to ensure that such care is in fact being provided?

Bibliography

Abse, L. (1979) 'Mend not end', *Sunday Telegraph*, 11 March.

Berfenstam, R. and William-Olsson, I. (1973) *Early Child Care in Sweden* (London: Gordon and Breach).

Brazelton, T. B. (1969) *Infants and Mothers: Differences in Development* (New York: Delacorte Press).

Brown, C. (1954) *My Left Foot* (London: Secker and Warburg).

Butler, N., Goldstein, H. and Ross, E. (1972) 'Cigarette smoking in pregnancy – its influence on birth weight and perinatal mortality', *British Medical Journal*, vol. 2, pp. 127–30.

Carlson, E. R. (1952) *Born That Way* (Evesham: Arthur James).

Clausen, J. A. (1978) 'American research on the family and socialization', *Children Today*, vol. 7, no. 2, pp. 7–10, 46.

Crellin, E., Pringle, M. K. and West, P. (1971) *Born Illegitimate* (Slough: NFER).

Department of Education and Science (1978) *Special Educational Needs* (Warnock Report) (London: HMSO).

Department of Health and Social Security (1976) *Fit for the Future* (Court Report) (London: HMSO).

Department of Health and Social Security (1977) *Prevention and Health: Reducing the Risk* (London: HMSO).

Department of the Environment (1973) *Children at Play* (London: HMSO).

Emery, A. E. H. (1977) 'Genetic counselling – its genetic and social implication', in R. Chester and J. Peel (eds), *Equalities and Inequalities in Family Life* (London: Academic Press).

Ferri, E. (1976) *Growing Up in a One-Parent Family* (Slough: NFER).

Fogelman, K. (ed.) (1976) *Britain's Sixteen-Year-Olds* (London: National Children's Bureau).

Franklin, A. W. (ed.) (1978) *Child Abuse – Prediction, Prevention and Follow-Up* (Edinburgh: Churchill Livingstone).

Goldstein, J., Freud, A. and Solnit, A. J. (1973) *Beyond the Best Interests of the Child* (New York: Free Press).

Hirsh, S. P. and Levin, K. (1978) 'How love begins between parent and child,' *Children Today*, vol. 7, no. 2, pp. 2–6, 47.

Home Office (1979) *Marriage Matters* (London: HMSO).

Jackson, R. H. (ed.) (1977) *Children, the Environment and Accidents* (London: Pitman Medical).

Kempe, R. S. and Kempe, C. (1978) *Child Abuse* (London: Fontana/Open Books).

Lamb, M. E. (ed.) (1976) *The Role of the Father in Child Development* (New York: Wiley).

Newson, J. and Newson, E. (1970) *Four Year Olds in the Urban Community* (Harmondsworth: Penguin).

Pilling, D. (1973) *The Child with Cerebral Palsy: Social, Emotional and Educational Adjustment* (Slough: NFER).

Pilling, D. (1973) *The Child with Spina Bifida: Social, Emotional and Educational Adjustment* (Slough: NFER).

Pilling, D. and Pringle, M. K. (1978) *Controversial Issues in Child Development* (London: Elek).

Pringle, M. K. (1964a) *The Emotional and Social Adjustment of Blind Children* (Slough: NFER).

Pringle, M. K. (1964b) *The Emotional and Social Adjustment of Physically Handicapped Children* (Slough: NFER).

Pringle, M. K. (ed.) (1965) *Investment in Children* (London: Longman).

Pringle, M. K. (1978) 'Towards the prediction and prevention of child abuse', *Bulletin of the British Psychological Society*, vol. 31 (May) p. 185.

Pringle, M. K. (1980) *The Needs of Children*, 2nd edn (London: Hutchinson).

Pringle, M. K. and Fiddes, O. (1970) *The Challenge of Thalidomide* (London: Longman).

Prosser, H. (1976) *Perspectives on Residential Child Care* (Slough: NFER).

Pugh, G. (1980) (ed.) *Preparation for Parenthood: Some Current Initiatives and Thinking* (London: National Children's Bureau).

Rossi, A. S. (1977) 'A biosocial perspective on parenting', *Daedalus*, vol. 106, no. 2, pp. 1–31.

Rutter, M. *et al.* (1979) *15,000 Hours* (London: Open Books).

Sadler, J. (1972) *Children and Road Safety* (London: HMSO).

Sandels, S. (1975) *Children in Traffic*, rev. ed (London: Elek).

Schaffer, H. R. (ed.) (1977) *Studies in Mother–Infant Interaction* (London: Academic Press).

Vowles, M., Pethybridge, R. J. and Brimblecombe, F. S. W. (1975) 'Congenital malformations in Devon; their incidence, age and primary source of detection', in G. McLachlan (ed.) *Bridging in Health* (Oxford University Press).

Whitehead, L. (1977) 'Early parenthood', *Concern*, vol. 24, pp. 28–30.

Wynn, A. (1976) 'Health care systems for pre-school children', *Proceedings of the Royal Society of Medicine*, vol. 69, no. 5, pp. 340–3.

Wynn, M. (1976) 'A policy for prevention: health care for every child', *Concern*, vol. 21, pp. 9–12.

Wynn, M. and Wynn, A. (1972–3) 'Using maternity benefits for preventive purposes', *Concerns*, vol. 11, pp. 13–16.

Wynn, M. and Wynn, A. (1977) *The Prevention of Preterm Birth: an Introduction to Some European Developments Aimed at the Prevention of Handicap* (London: Foundation for Education and Research in Child-Bearing).

Younghusband, D., Birchall, D., Davie, R. and Pringle, M. Kellmer (1971) *Living With Handicap* (London: National Children's Bureau).

11

Changing Roles for Parents and Professionals

Mia Kellmer Pringle

It is now widely accepted that physical, emotional and intellectual development are closely inter-related; and that this development in turn depends on the interaction of a broad range of genetic and environmental conditions. Among the latter, the family is the most basic and continuing influence, with the neighbourhood and school being next in importance.

Preventive medicine made major strides forward when doctors began to pool knowledge and share expertise with other professional groups. Chemists, physicists, pharmacologists, nutritionists, public health engineers and many others contributed to creating a healthier environment by ensuring a pure water supply, sewerage, clean air, uncontaminated food, etc. In the same way, the key professions concerned with promoting the optimal all-round development of children – paediatricians, health visitors and teachers – must pool knowledge and improve co-ordination both with each other and with related professional workers, such as obstetricians, psychologists, psychiatrists, social workers, speech therapists, planners and architects. Only then will a major move forward towards prevention become possible.

If positive child care and constructive education are to be an effective investment in children, then existing services need to be reshaped to become more comprehensive and more forward looking. Also, they need to be not only child-centred but family-orientated. If it is true that the grosser forms of need have largely been eliminated from our welfare society, then it is likely there will be fewer simple problems. Instead the matrix of difficulties will tend to grow more complex and more subtle. This demands increasing professionalism and thus correspondingly higher standards of training. It also makes it more unlikely than ever, that any one service or any one type of professional specialist has 'The key'. Rather, answers must be sought in evolving new patterns of co-operation. (Pringle, 1965)

Though some fifteen years have elapsed since this was written, it still needs saying today. Perhaps lip service is now more generally paid to the need for such co-operation but in practice very slow progress is being made towards achieving this apparently agreed objective.

Barriers to co-operation

At the simplest level, it takes more time and trouble to share information, consult others and discuss possible courses of action than to take decisions oneself. Added difficulties relate to the fact that patterns and hours of work are very different: teachers, unlike doctors and social workers, are not normally available for consultation in the evening or at week-ends; and they have much longer holidays than most doctors or social workers, so that during these periods they are also not available.

Next, the relative prestige or public esteem of medicine, education and social work broadly reflects both the state of knowledge and the importance each of these professions has for the well-being of society. Only doctors hold within their power decisions of life and death; also everyone requires their ministrations at some time or other. The education service too is used by everyone, being compulsory during a major part of children's lives. In contrast, social work intervention is generally associated in the public mind with combating social inadequacy or failure, though this may have become less so since the reorganisation of social services. Inevitably too, the comparative status of these professions is affected by their very different standards and levels of training: in both the medical and teaching professions, all practitioners must have obtained recognised qualifications, which take years to acquire. In contrast, the majority of social workers (that is, 65 per cent) were still untrained in 1978.

At an even more fundamental level, there are differences in values, approach, attitudes and even terminology used. These are reflected in the different reactions experienced by an individual depending on whether s/he is a patient, pupil/student or client.

Nevertheless, there are signs of change. As minimal health and educational standards have now virtually been achieved for the majority, this is raising two basic questions: can the minority also be enabled to reach at least such minimal standards; and how can optimal levels be attained by the majority since these are required not only for continued technological and scientific progress but also – and more importantly – for the fulfilment of each individual's potential? To find the answers to these questions may serve to break down some of the barriers to co-operation because to do so needs a breakthrough in knowledge which is likely to require a fusing of medical, educational, psychological and sociological understanding.

Changing concepts and converging aims

In the past, the three key professions were largely orientated towards diseases or deficiencies. Medicine aimed at curing the sick, education at eradicating ignorance, and social work at rehabilitating social failures. Gradually a change has been taking place and its direction seems to be similar in the three professional fields. Positive good health, the education of the 'whole' child, and the strengthening of the individual in relation to society in order to cope with social stress are becoming the main aims of professional attention. This convergence of professional aims, with its emphasis on normality and the enhancement of human potential, while not a necessary precondition of co-operation, might well facilitate the process.

At the same time, it has become more widely accepted that 'vulnerable' children and their families are usually known to the doctors, teachers and social workers in an area; and that they pose complex and often inter-related problems to the various services. Thus co-operation might develop most fruitfully and readily in relation to this group in the population which may well comprise as high a proportion as 20 per cent of all families.

Another area of converging aims is training, particularly in relation to the special needs of children. Recent official reports, such as *Fit for the Future* (DHSS, 1976) and *Special Educational Needs* (DES, 1978), have stressed the vital role of specialised post-basic training; in social work, too, voices are beginning to be heard demanding specialisation. During advanced training, that is after basic training followed by practical experience, and during refresher courses may well be the most appropriate stage to include a common core, child-centred curriculum aimed at promoting interprofessional understanding and co-operation.

However, making claims for expertise and functions which not only go beyond the professional competence of a particular group but also threaten to assume that of another, inevitably undermines the willingness of the latter to co-operate. Examples are the recommendations that paediatricians should be responsible for dealing with every form of developmental delay, including learning difficulties, social, emotional and behavioural problems as well as the counselling of adolescents, sex education and preparation for parenthood (as argued in the Court Report, *Fit for the Future*); or the assumption that the social or even psychological functioning of the family, including violence to and by children, and the whole field of delinquency and intermediate treatment fall into the domain of social work.

Perhaps it is such claims which lead to fears that the pooling of knowledge and sharing of expertise may result in a harmful blurring of professional identities or to the violation of confidentiality. None of the above considerations questions that each profession will retain and develop further its own skills and body of theoretical knowledge. However, the whole issue of the confidentiality of records and of information is having to be faced on a much wider front. This is because all authority and all public services are being challenged by a demand for greater openness and accountability. Indirectly this may in fact serve to reduce interprofessional barriers.

Future directions

Some signposts to the way in which developments are moving can already be discerned. For example, health visitors are becoming attached to general practice; social workers are being assigned to groups of schools; some teachers are working with pre-school handicapped or disadvantaged children and their parents by acting as home visitors; health and sex education in schools is being undertaken not only by teachers themselves but contributions are being made by doctors, health visitors, psychologists and psychiatrists; and a variety of local co-ordinating committees and joint planning teams are being set up to foster a more co-operative and integrated approach by the professions most directly involved.

These initiatives are, however, neither as systematic and far-reaching nor as widespread and comprehensive as is necessary if all children and their families are to benefit. Far too many still slip through the mesh of available services. Far too often needs are discovered too late, so that the opportunity for prevention and optimal intervention is frequently missed. Whenever this becomes clearly, even tragically, obvious – whether it be the delayed discovery of deafness in a pupil who had been unjustifiably labelled mentally backward or the irreversible injury to a battered baby – it is staff turnover and poor communication which are invariably blamed.

Yet detailed investigation almost always shows that for a considerable time there had been parental concern or early warning signs from the child, or both, which had not been taken sufficiently seriously or heeded sufficiently early. Appointing more staff, exchanging more reports and establishing more co-ordinating committees are unlikely to provide the fundamental remedies which are required. These remedies are, I believe, to be found in the acceptance and adoption of three principles: that the care and education of children must become a truly shared task between parents and professionals; that, in consequence, the role of the 'expert' must change; and that prevention must become everyone's concern and be given top priority.

Parents and professionals as partners

The rise of professionalism in the field of child development has – inadvertently – undermined to some extent the confidence of parents in their own ability to know and to cope. The fact that the different professional workers do not speak with one voice and may even give conflicting advice, has further contributed to parental uncertainty, as has the general climate of a fading faith in religious and moral imperatives. In a world which is uncertain not only where it is going but where it wants or ought to go, bringing up children has become a more difficult task than before.

Professional workers on their part far too often underestimate parental knowledge and insight – a failing shared alike by many a doctor, psychologist, teacher, social worker and therapist. Such an attitude is inevitably communicated to parents when they are seeking advice and help. This will contribute to their inability to give a fully adequate account of the reasons for their concern.

Additional reasons are that laymen tend to be somewhat in awe of professional experts; that in unfamiliar surroundings most people are liable to have difficulty in marshalling their thoughts; and that special interviews and examinations are likely to engender stress and anxiety, which in turn make one appear less competent. These reactions in turn serve to confirm the professional workers' attitudes, leading them to underestimate parental understanding. And so both sides are locked in a mutually reinforcing circle of misapprehension, to the detriment of the child's well-being.

The needs of 'new' parents   What, then, ought to be done? Primarily to bring about a change in attitudes and expectations so as to readjust the perspectives of both sides. Parental confidence will have to be restored by a variety of means, based wherever possible on research evidence. Examples are the recently available knowledge of the vital role performed by the mother during the earliest weeks and months of a baby's life in helping him to build his first relationship; and the essential part which her sensitive, though often intuitive, awareness and understanding play in fostering a mutually enjoyable interaction which in turn promotes the baby's emotional, social and intellectual development.

The birth of the first baby marks an important period of change in the relationship and life-style of the couple. These changes have profound personal, financial and social implications. Parenthood demands the development of new roles for each partner; it brings with it different satisfactions and dissatisfactions; it imposes wide-ranging constraints on the couple's freedom of movement, leisure time and independence, as well as on all the minutiae of their life.

Both the new mother and the new father have to cope with changes in the way they see themselves and each other, while the way they are seen by others will also be altered. All these changes may generate major stress, resulting in maternal anxiety and depression as well as having an adverse effect on the marital relationship. While the couple will have been expecting changes to accompany their new status, they are much more likely to have anticipated the novelty and joys of becoming parents, while being little prepared for the negative aspects. Chief among these are the anxiety, uncertainty and sense of responsibility for a completely helpless, vulnerable human being, made worse by the sheer physical tiredness, if not exhaustion, of the first few weeks.

At present hardly any help is given to a couple to anticipate the range of likely changes and their impact on their whole way of life. Nor are they provided with any support while learning to cope with them, unless they are fortunate enough to have relatives, particularly their own parents, living nearby who are able to spare time to be with them. Furthermore, such an awareness and understanding should ideally be created before a couple decides to have a child so that their decision to do so is better informed than it all too often tends to be now.

Of course, some preparation is given in antenatal groups and parent-craft classes but even so, the emotional, social and psychological strains and stresses experienced by new parents are relatively neglected. Work is urgently required to explore how to promote anticipation and awareness and how best to provide emotional support.

Development guide   Entering simple details of growth in a 'Baby Book' is already quite popular. Some parents are likely to find a more systematic tool such as the Development Guide for 0-to 5-year-olds a more useful aid. This has been designed and produced by the National Children's Bureau. The guide offers an observational framework and if completed at regular intervals, provides a cumulative picture of a child's progress over time. Parental and in particular maternal confidence will be encouraged by a recognition of the vast amount of knowledge about a young child's abilities and weaknesses that is acquired through daily close, intimate and prolonged contact. Because the guide makes this knowledge more systematic and overt, it helps to increase both the parents' natural interest in the child's growth and their own self-assurance.

By using the guide regularly, parents will be more certain of how the child is progressing and they will also become more aware when development is slower in any one area of growth. Giving more stimulation and opportunities in this particular direction may well lead to a quickening pace of progress; this in turn will increase the mother's confidence in the effectiveness of her care. If such additional stimulation fails to have the desired result, then she will feel more justified in seeking expert help. Moreover having available the cumulative, documented evidence provided by the Development Guide should enable her to set out more convincingly the reasons for her anxiety, when seeing a specialist.

Complementing the parental role   On the part of professionals, the change of attitudes and expectations which is required relates to the recognition and acceptance of three facts. To begin with, the great majority of parents do not in the first place usually turn to professionals for advice but to their relations, friends and neighbours; only when seriously worried do they seek expert help.

Secondly, parental knowledge of the child is an essential complement to any specialist assessment. However skilled and experienced a diagnostician, however adequate the methods and tests used in paediatric, psychological or other specialist investigations, the time available is limited. Moreover, faced with a stranger, most probably in strange surroundings, a young child is unlikely to behave normally, quite apart from being affected by the unease, if not anxiety, felt by his mother in this situation. Yet a knowledge of the child's habitual behaviour in familiar circumstances is indispensable to complement the picture obtained in the specialist assessment of his all-round abilities and disabilities, if any.

Thirdly – except for the tiny minority who require long-term hospitalisation, residential schooling or other institutional treatment – for the vast majority of children it is the parents who have the major responsibility for their care and, during the pre-school years, their education as well. Of course, when there is serious developmental delay or markedly deviant growth, the expertise of highly trained professionals will always be essential, both for assessment and treatment. But their role is different from and can never supplant the task of those who have overall charge of and responsibility for the child's daily and continuous care.

Once a suspected handicap or disorder has been confirmed, then a remedial programme is likely to be required to reverse as far as possible any adverse effects and to minimise future developmental consequences. Only by taking parents fully into their confidence and by treating them as equal partners, can experts give them the confidence and the support for coping with children who have special needs. The greater the parents' awareness of what is required, the better they will be able to act on specialist advice and to carry out a programme which ultimately depends on their understanding and co-operation.

Teachers similarly need to accept and indeed welcome parents as partners. Once children start compulsory schooling, there is still a tendency in many a school to make parents feel unwanted. Those who were themselves poor scholars or disliked school for other reasons, are in any case likely to fight shy of making contact with teachers of their own accord. Yet evidence has been accumulating to show the influential role played by parental involvement in a child's educational progress. This is as true for achievement generally as it is for the success of compensatory programmes for disadvantaged pupils. While progressive thinking now aims to bring parents into a much closer relationship with their children's schooling and to promote parental understanding of new teaching methods, these are only first steps on the road to fostering a real partnership.

The changing role of professionals

If parents are to be accepted as full partners, then the role as well as the attitude of the 'expert' must change. S/he must translate into practical recognition the fact that it is the parents who play by far the most important part in the care and education of their children, particularly during the vital early years; that most care deeply for their well-being and development; but because child-rearing is a complex and challenging task, many parents become anxious at times about the significance of a problem and concerned whether their handling of it is appropriate. Consequently the first change required is that parental anxiety must always be taken seriously even if in the event it turns out to be a reflection of inexperience, self-doubt or exhaustion. In such cases a willingness to listen, to offer reassurance and guidance may be all that is required. Hence rather than 'prescribing' what is to be done, the expert should promote and support more confident parenting.

Potentially parents are the best 'detectors' of handicap. More attention should be paid to that rather maligned sixth sense, 'maternal instinct', because it is often the mother who has the first suspicion that all is not well with her child. To be told either 'not to worry' or that the child will 'grow out of it' is doing a disservice, if for no other reason than that such advice is unlikely to allay her anxiety which itself may have an adverse effect on the child's emotional development.

Alternatively, the worries expressed may not be directly related to the child but may be due to the mother missing the daily companionship of adults, previously enjoyed at work, or to loneliness due to moving to a new area, or to unsuitable housing conditions, or to marital difficulties. Then the professional task would be to give reassurance about the normality of the child's development, to help the mother to recognise the underlying problem and to discuss possible remedies with her. These may include putting her in touch with other young mothers in the area; encouraging her to set up an informal group if none exists in the neighbourhood; suggesting some new interest, perhaps through evening classes; putting her into touch with other relevant services, such as the social services and housing departments of the local authority, marriage guidance counselling, and the like.

The second change of practice required relates to children in whom some developmental delay or handicap is discovered. For too long has the fallacy of the simple, single handicap, and hence diagnosis by one specialist, been allowed to continue. In fact the simple, single handicap is rare, if it ever existed. For one thing, unless diagnosed and treated early, even minor physical disabilities may become complicated by secondary educational or emotional difficulties. For another, there are often consequential additional handicaps; for example, profound deafness inevitably affects speech and language development, resulting in barriers of communication which then lead to social difficulties.

Also in a society which sets great store on 'normality', the deviant child and his family need much support to face and cope with the fact of his/her being different, in addition to practical aids, such as wheelchairs, hoists and other modifications to the home.

Last, but by no means least, there may now be more children with multiple disabilities. While advances in medical knowledge have drastically reduced, or even entirely eliminated, the incidence of certain defects, they are on the other hand enabling a greater number of severely damaged children with multiple disabilities – such as those with spina bifida – to survive. For these reasons a diagnostic examination by one specialist is inadequate, even for an apparently uncomplicated single handicap. How best to meet the child's special needs cannot be decided upon without a whole range of information additional to the nature of the disability itself: the child's emotional, social and intellectual development must be known prior to planning his future; family relationships and material circumstances, such as income and suitability of housing, must be explored; and the school environment as well as the child's educational achievements must be taken into consideration.

A once-and-for-all diagnostic examination is also an unrealistic and inadequate procedure. Even with a comprehensive assessment it is essential to have a follow-up investigation to monitor whether the recommendations were implemented and if so, whether they proved to be successful. A follow-up is also necessary because a child's needs are likely to change over time as are family structure or circumstances.

Comprehensive assessment   Thus what is required in cases of special needs – whether these are physical, social, emotional, intellectual or a combination of these – is a comprehensive assessment by a multidisciplinary team with the focus on the child and his family. Its aim would be to plan a detailed programme for the care, education and treatment of the child, to be carried out by the parents, complemented and supplemented by teachers, social workers, doctors and appropriate specialists. The success of the programme should be regularly monitored and if need be, revised in the light of a full reassessment.

The third change of practice follows from the assessment procedure just outlined. On the one hand the parents would be quite free to discuss their child with any member of the team, each of whom should encourage them to ask questions to enable them to play their part better in the assessment and treatment. On the other hand, for some this could prove a rather confusing process. Hence it would be desirable for one member of the professional team to act as 'link-man and interpreter'. This idea was first suggested in the Bureau's report *Living with Handicap* in 1970 and in 1978 the Warnock Committee (DES, 1978) made a similar proposal for a 'named person'.

S/he would ensure that the parents understand the findings and recommendations as well as their own part in the future care, education and treatment of their child; that they have a focal point for asking questions and raising any problems at a later stage; that records are brought up to date from time to time, and passed on to others, suitably edited if need be; and that children are recalled according to decisions taken originally or because of unforeseen developments.

In summary, then, the role of the professional practitioner will become primarily that of an educator, catalyst, enabler and diagnostician providing support, guidance, know-how and back-up services but leaving the major task of care and education to the parents or those who stand *in loco parentis*, rather than usurping parental responsibilities.

The changing role of parents and the community

The beginnings of a new trend are reflected in the rapid growth of parental self-help movements during the past twenty years or so. It started when parents of handicapped children felt so dissatisfied with the lack of suitable educational and treatment provision that they banded together, determined to improve matters. And so the National Society for Mentally Handicapped Children, The Spastics Society, the National Association for Deaf/Blind and Rubella Children, the National Society for Autistic Children, and many others came into being.

The demonstrable success of the combined strength of such minority groups probably encouraged the growth of self-help movements among parents generally. Among these, the quite remarkable success of the Pre-school Playgroups Association is the most outstanding example, but many others, such as the National Association for the Welfare of Children in Hospital, have brought about very considerable changes in practice, sometimes despite determined professional doubts if not actual opposition.

The impetus of this movement is still continuing. Part of its strength derives from the fact that in addition to the national organisations, there are in many cases locally-based support groups run by parents for parents. Among the more recent developments are the National Foster Care Association.

The basic significance of these self-help movements would seem to be twofold. First, sooner or later all of them turn to professional workers for advice, guidance and support. But when they do so it is within the context of a redefined relationship of self-confidence and partnership. The determination to help themselves has remained their strength and driving force, inspired by the aim to improve the standards of care, education and treatment in the services available to their children.

Secondly, these self-help movements may well signal a real return to community care. The latter has become a fashionable slogan to which at present much lip service is paid by official voices. In fact, however, the community, or more concretely and realistically, women in the community have always shouldered the main burden of caring: for children, for the handicapped, the sick and the old. Hitherto they have been taken for granted, simply being expected to do this while sacrificing their chance of marriage or a career; without proper financial recompense and without adequate professional or even home-help support. Moreover the burden of low income, bad housing and insufficient food always bears heaviest on women who put the needs of their children before their own.

By generating self-help movements, by mobilising young people as volunteers and, in future, by harnessing to a greater extent the energies of the retired, redundant and unemployed, a renewed sense of mutual involvement in the welfare of one's neighbourhood could be created. Above all, it must include giving practical help of all kinds to care-giving women so as to lighten their load of unremitting responsibility for immature, aged or infirm dependants. In this way a true spirit of community care will be fostered, rooted in and springing from individuals who value self-reliance, practical action and a measure of independence from authority and from professional expertise. In the process many may discover or rediscover that the 'gift relationship' enriches not only the recipient but also the giver (Titmuss, 1971).

People living in the neighbourhood of an institution can also help to improve the quality of life for the 'inmates' by regular contact. Examples are the 'uncle and aunt scheme' (at present largely defunct) whereby children growing up in long-term residential care or in hospitals are visited as well as taken out by individual men and women willing to make a reliable commitment to do so over a period of time; or the 'visiting granny scheme' for young children in hospital whose own parents are not able to visit daily and for whom even a short period in a frightening, often pain-inflicting environment can be deeply disturbing without the solace of a parent substitute with time to spare for individual attention.

The principle of mutual support and self-help can also be extended to those traditionally viewed as in need of care from others. For example, in a mental deficiency hospital the adult patients were allowed to 'adopt' a child patient and were encouraged to perform simple tasks of parental care for their charges. As a result the morale, self-confidence and general capacity to cope increased among both adults and children. Initiated and guided by professional workers, the scheme was found to improve the motivation and quality of life for all concerned.

Thus it seems that the concept of community involvement and community care could well be encouraged to flourish within the confines of residential establishments themselves. Similarly, new self-help movements are now growing apace, initiated by people afflicted by a wide range of illnesses and handicapping conditions. A spirit of disenchantment with professionalism and the bureaucratisation of the helping services – from hospitals to social services – appears to have kindled a determination to find knowledge, understanding and strength through mutual support and self-help. So the time seems ripe for 'a radical programme of action research into ways to give ordinary people the opportunity to discover new dimensions to caring' (Volunteer Centre, 1976).

Community-based family centres

Might an actual physical base help to foster and develop this new focus on a partnership between parents and professional workers, and on self-help movements generally? In the present economic climate splendid new buildings are clearly not a practical possibility but arguably more 'homely', previously 'lived in' premises may well be preferable anyhow. For example, due to the drop in the birth-rate, many primary schools will have to be closed down and put to new use. To renovate and adapt them would be much less costly than purpose-built centres. Disused churches, empty shops and stores might similarly lend themselves to conversions.

What facilities and services should such community-based family centres provide? They should be multipurpose, ranging from offering a meeting point for purely social and recreational purposes to making available advice, counselling and referral to specialised agencies if required. All members of the family should have ready access to it and the mixing of ages would be a matter of deliberate policy to foster the kind of community involvement discussed earlier. There might be a pre-school playgroup, toy library and after school hours play and hobby facilities available for children; a snack bar, meeting rooms and book shop for adults; all based on a policy of ready intermingling of activities and age groups. Except for a small staff, the running of the centre would be in the hands of the community itself.

The advice, counselling and referral services would be staffed by a team of professional workers from the health, social services and education authorities. Operating on an informal drop-in basis would remove the all too frequent barriers to seeking early help, including the fear and stigma of being apparently unable to cope. The emphasis would be on normality and prevention rather than on crisis intervention, disease or treatment. Use would be made both of other parents who have had similar concerns and difficulties, and of volunteers from the community. The professional expert's role would be that of an adviser, facilitator and educator, using the term in its broadest sense; his main task being to help people to learn to help themselves and to make the best use of available facilities and services.

What would be the distinguishing features of such community-based family centres? To begin with, they would create a welcoming, open and accepting atmosphere; next, they would be informal, flexible and ready to adapt to changing needs and circumstances; also they would be easily accessible to the people they are serving – in other words, within pram-pushing, wheelchair or an old person's walking distance.

Basically these ideas are not new. Before the war, the Peckham Experiment (Pearse and Crocker, 1943) pioneered the concept of positive family health – both physical and mental – to be promoted and studied by biologists. Current schemes designed to involve whole communities in this way are described earlier by Colin Ward. 'High Street Advice Centres' and 'Education Shops' have been called for by the Advisory Centre for Education and the National Educational Research and Development Trust, which established some as pilot experiments. Wall has argued (1977) that the school is 'ideally placed to be the focus of much, if not all, the community action concerned with the prevention of difficulties, problems and breakdown, and with the constructive control of the impact of change. Moreover, as educational concern stretches back into early childhood and forward to the continuing education of adults, the education system becomes increasingly comprehensive in its responsibilities.'

So far, however, neighbourhood centres of any kind are extremely thin on the ground. There are even fewer that adopt the wide, preventive aims outlined earlier together with a deliberate policy of involving members of the community they serve in planning and running the centre as equal partners with the professionals. Yet there can be little doubt that such family centres would be more cost effective than the extremely expensive institutions which society provides for juvenile delinquents for example. Though these have been shown to do little more than contain them for a short time (recidivism runs at about 70 per cent for all the different types) nevertheless more are in the pipeline at a cost of between £10 000 to £20 000 per annum per place.

If community-based, multipurpose family centres became as common as shops, pubs and bingo halls; if early prevention and intervention were to be adopted as a national policy and translated into service provision by local government and the health authorities; if the self-help movement and voluntary participation were given the fullest recognition and support; then it might well prove possible to improve the quality of life for our children and the community at large in a way which may seem utopian today.

Bibliography

Bronfenbrenner, U. (1975) 'Nature with nurture: a reinterpretation of the evidence', in A. Montagu (ed.), *Race and I.Q.* (New York: Oxford University Press).
Department of Education and Science (1978) *Special Educational Needs* (Warnock Report) (London: HMSO).
Department of Health and Social Security (1976) *Fit for the Future* (Court Report) (London: HMSO).
Department of Health and Social Security (1977) *Prevention and Health: Reducing the Risk* (London: HMSO).
Fogelman, K. and Goldstein, H. (1976) 'Social factors associated with changes in educational attainment between 7 and 11 years of age', *Educational Studies*, vol. 2, no. 2, pp. 95–109.
Liffman, M. (1978) *Power for the Poor* (London: Allen and Unwin).
National Children's Bureau (1977) *Development Guide 0–5 Years* (London: National Children's Bureau).
Newson, J. and Newson, E. (1977) *Perspectives on School at Seven Years Old* (London: Allen and Unwin).
Pearse, I. H. and Crocker, L. H. (1943) *The Peckham Experiment* (London: Allen and Unwin).
Pilling, D. and Pringle, M. K. (1978) *Controversial Issues in Child Development* (London: Elek).
Pringle, M. K. (ed.) (1965) *Investment in Children* (London: Longman).
Pringle, M. K. (1971) *Deprivation and Education*, 2nd ed (London: Longman).

Pringle, M. K. (1978) 'The Bureau's development guide for 0–5 year olds', *Concern*, vol. 27, pp. 5–8.

Pringle, M. K. (1980) *The Needs of Children*, 2nd edn (London: Hutchinson).

Pringle, M. K. and Naidoo, S. (1975) *Early Child Care in Britain* (London: Gordon and Breach).

Pugh, G. and Russell, P. (1977) *Shared Care: Support Services for Families with Handicapped Children* (London: National Children's Bureau).

Titmuss, R. M. (1971) *The Gift Relationship: From Human Blood to Social Policy* (London: Allen and Unwin).

Volunteer Centre (1976) *Annual Report 1976/7* (Berkhamstead: Volunteer Centre).

Wall, W. D. (1977) *Constructive Education for Adolescents* (London: Harrap).

12

Concluding Questions

Mia Kellmer Pringle

To ensure a fairer future for all our children a number of crucial questions must be faced and answers decided upon not only by parents and professionals but by a consensus reached by society as a whole. They are to do with choices, priorities and policies. Many stem from research findings about the needs and development of children but in the last resort, all the issues require judgements to be made and preferences to be determined whenever there is some incompatibility or even conflict between the best interests of adults and the young.

The ten questions raised here are, of course, by no means exhaustive but I have singled out those which seem to me crucial and of long-term practical significance. Most of them arise from the conditions, problems and dilemmas discussed in the preceding chapters.

Can a greater national commitment to the well-being of children be created?

This question is perhaps the most fundamental of all since it relates to the quality of life itself. Our society is now coming face to face with the consequences of unplanned and impersonal technological, scientific and industrial progress; of the ever more competitive greed of a consumer society; of the wasteful squandering of our natural resources, including human potential; and of the price exacted by the rat-race on our sense of values as well as on our physical and mental health.

Somehow we have come to believe that our standard of living should not only rise but continue to do so. Consequently, we have grown to worship material success. Is it worth it? Do contentment and personal fulfilment require a fundamental rethinking of what makes life worth living?

Need we find a different commitment – a commitment with a more human face? A socially fairer and juster society means a community which no longer tolerates that amidst general affluence one child in sixteen grows up in squalor and deprivation; and that valuable human potential is destined to remain tragically and wastefully unfulfilled among a sizeable minority of tomorrow's parents.

Can such a change in public attitudes be brought about? There are many voices ready to dismiss this possibility on the grounds of original sin; or the complexity of the human personality; or the belief that the urge to compete is stronger than the wish to co-operate; to name just a few of the arguments brought to bear. But surely, there can be no certainty of failure unless we first attempt to bring about such a change with a whole-hearted commitment and belief in its viability. After all, encouraging changes in public attitudes have been achieved in other areas, such as more humane views about the mentally sick, the handicapped and law-breakers as well as more recently on environmental pollution and smoking.

Can the needs of children and the rights of women be reconciled?

There can be no doubt by now that a child's psychological development is profoundly and significantly influenced by the kind of care s/he receives. Though development is ultimately limited by biological and genetic factors, it is the quality of care that determines the extent to which all the infant's potentialities will eventually be realised. The essential ingredients of such care are unconditional affection and acceptance; appropriate and varied intellectual stimulation; and responsive interaction.

During the first three years of life, a dependable, consistent, warm, mutually satisfying and continuous relationship is crucial to optimal development. Most mothers find it rewarding to have the time to enjoy being closely involved in their child's rapid growth which takes place during these vital years. In turn this intimate and absorbing involvement is an important motivation which influences both the rate and quality of progress. Full-time maternal (or paternal for that matter) care is unique in the sense that it allows the mother time to develop sensitivity to her baby which then enables her to recognise and adapt to his/her very individual needs.

The women's liberation movement justifiably demands that equal rights be accorded in education, training, employment and career prospects as well as in marriage. By choosing to ignore one vital difference between the sexes, namely that only women can conceive and bear children, the movement has – wittingly or otherwise – brought about a serious devaluing of mothering and home-making as well as a misleadingly biased portrayal of young children. So much so that educated girls are made to feel that they are wasting their abilities if they are 'only a housewife and mother'.

This is doubly unfortunate. It deprives many a young woman of the sense of joy, pride and achievement when she creates a nurturing and happy environment for her family. And it misrepresents caring for infants and toddlers as boring and irksome instead of recognising that good mothering is an extremely skilled, challenging, demanding, responsible and vital job; in fact more responsible in the long term than most professional careers, let alone the routine jobs available to the vast majority of both men and women.

Surely there are no insuperable difficulties in enabling mothers (or fathers if a couple so wishes to arrange its family life) to devote four to ten years out of a potential working life span of altogether forty or more years to caring for their young children? The only obstacles at present are those created by a largely man-made and male-orientated labour market which finds it easier and more convenient to take a conservative, traditional view of women's place in and contribution to the work force.

Employers and trade unions alike refuse to acknowledge – or, more irresponsibly still, even fail to consider – the needs of young children. They gloss over the fact that high-quality day nurseries and creches are a very expensive provision and reject the evidence that group methods of care for under-threes are not the best way of meeting their needs. Though paying a child-care allowance or greatly increased child benefit would be less costly solutions, trade unions and the women's liberation movement object to them by arguing that they could be used as a means of 'pushing women back into the home'; they claim employers would find it easier to dismiss mothers without having a bad social conscience.

Surely the way to reconcile these differences should be to acknowledge that by bringing up a family a mother is performing a social and economic function which is every bit as important as any contribution she might have made and may again make to business, industry, commerce or the professions. She (and her husband) should be able to choose how to cope with the dual, and at times competing, demands of paid work outside the home and child-care responsibilities; and she should have the opportunity to make this choice free from economic, social or emotional pressures.

A policy for families or for children?

The importance of the family is now being given increasing emphasis in both public and political debate. Ideas such as a national voluntary family movement, a statutory family welfare commission, and the need for family impact statements to be mandatory in relation to all new legislation, are all based on two growing beliefs: first, that the well-being of families is vital to the well-being of society as a whole; and secondly, that in the past three or more decades the family has increasingly lost out, particularly in financial terms. To rectify the situation, it is argued, political pressure needs to be organised so that the family can establish its rightful claims and be heard amid the competing, powerful and effective voices of other special interest groups.

Could not an equally good, or even better, case be made for a policy for children? Critics of this proposal claim that surely what is good for the family must be good for children. For the majority this may well be true. However, the extent to which this is so has not yet been systematically explored, nor have the areas of potential conflict between the interests of parents and their offspring been seriously examined.

To my mind, it is preferable to frame a policy which places the major emphasis on the needs of children. First, because of hostility to government intervention; second, because of conflicting interests of parents and children; and third, because today's children will be tomorrow's citizens.

Hostility to government intervention

In democratic societies at least, there is resistance to, and indeed suspicion of, state interference in people's private lives. Adults are considered to be responsible for the way in which they conduct their personal affairs; and they can only be deprived of the liberty to do so in very specific, legally defined ways. This is so even when a man's

behaviour is blatantly irresponsible, such as gambling away most of his earnings, to the detriment of his family's welfare. It is arguable to what extent adults should be protected, either by legislation or by heavier taxation, against harming themselves, for example by drink or tobacco.

For children, however, the position is different. When parents or those *in loco parentis* fail to exercise their responsibilities adequately, then surely as the agent of society, government must intervene to ensure that their well-being is safeguarded. Of course, education and persuasion should be used first. But what if these fail? The issues are undoubtedly complex and delicate and there are no simple answers. But in arguing for a policy for children, the question of the individual's liberty assumes to my mind a different dimension.

Conflicting interests of parents and children

Children are totally dependent upon adults. They have no in-dependent voice, no vote and few rights in law. In fact, most laws are in the nature of directions and prohibitions, limiting their choices, although many are, of course, designed to protect their health and welfare. Adults, for example, can choose their place of work and have some influence on their working conditions. In contrast, children are forced to go to school, even when they are patently unhappy and failing to derive much benefit from their education; also they have no influence on the choice of school or class which they must attend.

This example also illustrates the fact that the interest of the paren does not necessarily coincide with that of the child. On the one hand compulsory school attendance frees the mother from her respons ibility for full-time care. Thus, it provides her with much more fre time for her own interests, including paid employment. On the oth hand, many five-year-olds are not ready for full-time educatic physically, emotionally, socially or intellectually, and in some cas on all four grounds. For them, part-time education or even postp ing it until they are more mature would be an advantage. In f Britain and a few of the Commonwealth countries are alone in world in making full-time schooling (that is, from 9 a.m. to 4 p compulsory from such an early age.

Another area of potential conflict between the interests of the and his parents is family size. On the one hand, the idea of a family appeals to many couples; moreover, some womer

happiest and healthiest during pregnancy and the early months of their baby's life. On the other hand, research shows that children develop less well if they grow up in a large, rather than a small, family. A family-centred policy would regard the number of children a couple chose to have as a private matter; and child benefit would be paid regardless of how many there are.

In contrast, a policy concerned with the best interests of children would make widely known the effects of family size on their development. Educational as well as fiscal means might be used in an attempt to change attitudes. Family planning services would be made available on a priority basis to those who already have one child. And child benefit and tax allowances could be designed in such a way as to give the greatest financial support for the first and second child while tailing off allowances for subsequent children.

The most dramatic as well as tragic conflicts of interests arise in relation to abused children. The vast majority of parents are, of course, deeply caring and concerned. A minority, however, show little real or continuous interest in the welfare of their children, and may actually harm them. In my view, there is little justification for striving to keep children with such parents or for letting them wait in public care for years in the hope that it may one day become possible to reunite them with their biological family. In the long-term interest of such children a permanent foster home, or better still adoption, seems to be the only viable alternative.

Yet it is argued that the natural parents have been as much sinned against as sinning since in many cases they themselves have experienced ill-treatment at the hands of their own parents or spouses; and that removing the child will make the adults' treatment and rehabilitation more difficult. This view not only gives priority to parental interests but acting on it also runs a high risk of perpetuating ill-treatment and abuse from one generation to another.

If the best long-term interests of the child were to become the main criteria for resolving conflicts between the well-being of parents and children respectively, then at least some rough justice would prevail. After all, children did not ask to be born: they require protection and have inevitably far less choice and freedom of action than is available to adults, at least in Western society. Hence it is justifiable to accord paramountcy to their needs.

Today's children – tomorrow's citizens

A policy for children would give practical recognition to the fact that they are the seedcorn of the future. Their development determines the fabric of tomorrow's society. Whether it will be more cohesive and more tolerant of racial and cultural differences; whether the incidence of mental stress, violence, vandalism and crime will increase or diminish; all these depend to a very considerable degree on the priority which we are willing to accord to meeting adequately the needs of growing children. The ability to care grows from having experienced loving care. In the long run, a policy for children will benefit parents too, though in the shorter term it may limit the degree of their choice and freedom to some extent.

Is there perhaps a need to have both a policy for the family and a policy for children? The case for the former has been argued convincingly in quite a few documents and statements, while the case for the latter is of more recent origin. There seems to be greater ambivalence about, if not hostility to, the idea of a policy for children. Partly this may be based on the by no means obsolete view of children as chattels and partly on the misconception that children are unable to articulate their views and feelings in a coherent, critical and constructive manner. Yet there is in fact evidence that they can do so and that the voices of children and adolescents are well worth listening to and taking into account.

Four examples must suffice. First, though physical chastisement for adults has been outlawed in Britain for many years now in prisons and borstals, as well as in the armed forces, corporal punishment continues to be exercised in all institutions catering for children, from schools to children's homes and community homes (formerly approved schools); even five-year-old infants and handicapped pupils are not exempt from this practice. While the opinions of teachers and other adults on this issue are well known and often heard, those of children are seldom sought nor given any weight. Yet their views are clear and well-defined (Fogelman, 1976; Page and Clark, 1977).

The second example relates to children of divorce whose feelings and attitudes are all too rarely taken into proper consideration when decisions about their future lives and in particular about custody are being made. Certainly, they often have strong views which may differ from those of the adults concerned.

The third example concerns children who are growing up in

residential care because their parents are unable or unwilling to look after them. A moving illustration of the clarity, insight, compassion and forcefulness of their views and concerns was well illustrated in a recent publication (Page and Clark, 1977).

The fourth example relates to children who are seriously neglected and ill-treated by their parents. Older children can show their feelings and reactions both through speaking out and by running away from home, that is, 'voting with their feet', as it were; even quite young children demonstrate in unmistakable ways their suffering, fear and terror in the presence of the abusing parent. Yet these reactions are all too often given insufficient weight when decisions are made about the short- or long-term future of such children.

Perhaps the main argument for a policy for children is one of values. 'A nation's compassion may be shown in its care for the disabled and those past work, but for evidence of its concern for its future (which also includes its capacity to exercise this compassion) we can only look at its care for its children' (Walley, 1972).

Financing the cost of children – personal luxury or public responsibility?

The relative financial position of parents compared with non-parents is worse today than it was forty years ago. This deterioration is due in part to the tax and welfare policies of successive governments, and in part to the increasing costs of rearing children (Parker, 1978). Fragmentation characterises the present system of family income support, benefit rates being tied to employment circumstances and other rather arbitrary distinctions, instead of the needs of children at different ages and stages of growth.

Insufficient recognition is being given to this situation and to the serious financial pressures facing families with dependent children. Nor is sufficient attention paid to the link between these pressures (which include poor housing and chronic ill-health) and the incidence, if not increase, in vandalism, truancy, delinquency and educational failure. Compared with the other EEC countries, Britain lags behind regarding family income support, welfare politics being dominated by the pensioner's lobby.

A recent report (Parker, 1978) claimed that

the post-war system of family income support, which from the outset lacked coherence, has been reduced by the events of 33 years to a jungle of contradictions and anomalies which endanger the very foundations of our society, and for which the Child Benefit Act in its present form offers no sure solution . . . We live in a patriarchal society, where the rights of children as equal citizens are studiously ignored.

Family income support means spreading the cost of rearing children between parents and non-parents. The case for it rests on two propositions. The first is that the home environment remains, and should remain, the chief influence in a child's life; and secondly, that family income is seldom related to family commitments. Without special support many a family sinks into poverty when the first child comes along and then the situation deteriorates with the birth of each subsequent infant.

Among the major recommendations made by the Outer Circle Policy Unit are the introduction of a new antenatal allowance for expectant mothers and generous but taxable child benefits. Phased into a system of tax reliefs they would

prevent hardship entirely, they would greatly reduce relative deprivation and, provided they were part of a co-ordinated tax and welfare system, they would encourage parental responsibility and self-reliance. By making work more profitable, and therefore more attractive, the whole economy would benefit . . . Family income support, if it is to be effective, cannot be done on the cheap but the long-term benefits are inestimable . . . it must be regarded as investment in the nation's most valuable resource, which is each future generation. Children, after all, are the wealth creators of tomorrow, upon whose efforts and abilities all our futures depend. (Parker, 1978)

Accepting this argument means accepting that the financial burden of raising children should no longer be regarded largely as the duty of parents alone but as a shared responsibility between society and those individuals who are willing to undertake this onerous task. Of course, monetary support can in no way fully compensate parents for inevitably long 'hours of duty', asocial hours and a lowered standard of living compared with childless couples. But choices have always to be paid for and there are, of course, many joys and rewards in raising a family for those who truly love children.

Can more rational priorities be encouraged?

As a society, we make paradoxical choices and adopt paradoxical priorities. Hearts and other organs are transplanted at very great cost but every year thousands of children are seriously hurt in preventable accidents. In 1968 more children died in Britain in fires alone than people were murdered, yet just one intensive and prolonged murder hunt probably costs more than the total amount spent annually on teaching parents about fire risks and prevention.

Though the earliest years of childhood are the most important for later development, we devote considerably more to older children. For example, for every £1 spent on children aged 7 to 11 years in primary schools, £14 is spent on a university student. Similarly, it is recognised that removal from home is the more traumatic the younger the child. Nevertheless, every week 500 children under five years of age come into care, many of them from single parents. Yet the supplementary allowance given to one-parent families is substantially less than it costs to provide substitute residential care for their children.

Nursery education provides a different kind of example. Due to

> a combination of central and local government regulations, the Inner London Education Authority will spend £690,000 in 1979/80 on measures to reduce the fire risks in educational buildings . . . but there is no record of a child being so much as singed in any day school in London by reason of the sort of thing that fire precautions deal with . . . Would spending the money on nursery school places for under-fives instead put life and limb in hazard? On the contrary. Children aged between three and five are very vulnerable at home. (Newsam, 1979)

Another example relates to the possibility of reallocating funds within the budget of a particular department. In education it could be used to redress the present relative neglect of the under-fives and of disadvantaged youngsters when compared with spending on sixth-formers. Even as small as a 2 per cent reallocation of funds could make an appreciable difference. The same is true regarding a switch of resources from residential provision for juvenile delinquents to developing community-based facilities instead.

Lastly, much prominence is given to minority groups, such as delinquents or drug addicts; comparatively little is heard about the thousands of children in our relatively affluent society who grow up emotionally neglected, or even rejected, and intellectually stunted. Yet they represent a much greater waste of human resources, a much larger pool of human misery.

Should uneconomic priorities be abandoned?

Probably the chief reason why we continue to accept uneconomical priorities and remain prepared to pay the most for the least effective provision is the lack of a coherent policy for children. Other reasons are that no one minister is charged with the task of co-ordinating and examining the implications of any policies or laws which may have an impact on the well-being of children; nor are government departments charged with bearing in mind the interests of families and the young in particular. A few examples will illustrate uneconomic priorities in a variety of policy areas.

Though child benefit is now paid for all children, the rate for the first-born should be much higher than that for subsequent children. It is the arrival of the first child which causes the most marked drop in parental income. Until then, the vast majority of women will have been in paid employment so that the couple enjoyed two incomes. Subsequently, only a tiny minority (some 6 per cent) return to full-time work outside the home before the child starts school. In addition, everything has to be bought for the first baby, from the pram and clothes to furniture and toys.

Another example relates to the care of under-threes. By 1978 the average capital cost of a place at a day nursery was about £4000 and the running cost about £1300 a year. Thus it is not only an expensive provision, but it is now generally accepted that group care cannot fully meet the needs of very young children. The two preferable alternative solutions would be far less costly yet much more beneficial to growth and development. If mothers of under-threes were paid even half the total cost of a day nursery place, many would choose to look after their young children themselves. The second alternative for those children whose mothers prefer to work full- or part-time (and whose husbands are unwilling or unable to provide the care required) would be placement with a child-minder. Currently this service is grossly undervalued and underpaid, the term itself and the average annual cost of about £250 being clear reflections of this fact. Properly trained and supported day foster mothers – a far more appropriate description – would be in every way a much more cost-effective form of substitute care.

In the educational field, recent studies – some new, some based on the re-analysis of old data – indicate that the wave of pessimism in the 1960s regarding the long-term beneficial effects of early intervention programmes for socially disadvantaged pre-school children was unjustified. When well-managed and run by a dedicated staff using a high-quality, well-planned curriculum, then such a programme does confer lasting advantages on young children over their peers who did not get this special help. Moreover, early intervention pays, not only in terms of educational and social benefits but in financial terms.

Parental involvement has proved to be a prerequisite (Weikart *et al.*, 1978). 'The combination of both classroom and home teaching was a central concept of the project and may have been the driving force behind its success.' Perhaps the most persuasive argument in the prevailing economic climate is that cost analysis suggests such programmes actually save money. For one thing, the pupils who participated did not require expensive special education as did those not in the programme. Then the projected lifetime earnings of the children involved in such programmes were calculated to be considerably higher than those of the controls since the former were more likely to finish.school and find decent jobs. 'Money invested in a year of pre-school "earned" interest in the form of benefits at the rate of $9\frac{1}{2}\%$ . . . What's good for children also appears to be of benefit to taxpayers' (Weber *et al.*, 1978).

Still in the educational field, the size of classes becomes smaller the older the pupils. Yet the older they are, the more they can learn by themselves under the teacher's guidance. In contrast, younger children require a great deal of individual attention while they are acquiring the basic skills. With classes of thirty-five pupils or more in primary schools, it is patently impossible to provide such attention. Consequently, a sizeable number remain educationally backward so that later on more costly remedial work and literacy programmes have to be provided for secondary school pupils and for adults.

In the field of substitute care, evidence is now incontestable that life in institutions has damaging effects on many of the inmates, be they hospital patients, borstal boys or children. Yet this most costly form of care continues to be used for ever-increasing numbers. Some £150 million is spent on residential facilities while only about £17 million is invested in day care. In other countries – for example Sweden – the position is reversed.

In the medical field, play in hospital is a simple example. The opportunity to play enables a child to cope better not only with the inevitable separation from home but also with the fear and pain as well as with the effects of surgical and other unpleasant procedures. Compared with the total costs of a hospital stay, the cost of a play leader is relatively cheap. Yet a significant proportion of hospitals fail to provide one.

A last example comes from the planning field. In cities, more space is allocated to car parks than to children's play facilities. Partly as a consequence, over 700 are killed on the roads each year and 15 000 seriously injured. Even ignoring the pain, grief and loss of life, the cost of providing long-term treatment, if not life-long care for the worst affected, is extremely high.

Uneconomic priorities are costly in human as well as in financial terms. Failure to provide adequate support and preventive services for all children means that later on much more expensive rehabilitation, treatment or punitive facilities have to be paid for. Surely the case for abandoning uneconomic priorities is incontrovertible?

Should preparation for parenthood be available for all young people?

There is at present only one subject which all schools are obliged to provide, namely religious education. Why this should continue to be so despite the prevailing climate of opinion and despite the demands of secularists, is a matter for speculation. Be this as it may, is there not a stronger case for making preparation for parenthood a required subject in all secondary schools since – at least on current showing – the vast majority of pupils will eventually become parents?

There are further arguments in support of such a proposal. First, there is evidence that where it is done well, pupils of all abilities find it absorbing to learn about child development and family life; this is perhaps of particular practical importance for bored or even alienated adolescents, too many of whom are opting out of school, whether merely mentally through lack of involvement or physically as well by becoming chronic truants.

Secondly, being 'creative and doing your own thing' has in recent years come to be elevated as a desirable and enviable life-style; at the same time, bringing up children has come to be portrayed as a boring, time-consuming and restricting activity. Yet, begetting and rearing the new generation is surely the most creative task of all – biologically, socially and emotionally – since without it there would be no future. To designate it as 'just being a job' is to undervalue it to the point of caricature, just as it is intellectually dishonest to portray any other creative job as invariably enjoyable, exciting and rewarding. All creative work involves hard effort, frustration, disappointment, tedium and at times even boredom. It is vital that a balanced and honest picture of parenthood be presented to adolescents so that when the time comes they can make an informed choice which is appropriate for them.

Thirdly, learning about human development, and children's development in particular, is likely to promote the adolescent's own personal maturation. Studying infancy and subsequent stages of growth enables young people to gain insight into their own past and family relationships, as well as to acquire some understanding of their future role as parents. Being themselves no longer children, but not fully accepted into the adult world either, they are fascinated and curious about both. The more factually yet imaginatively these worlds are portrayed to them, the more readily their intellectually awareness and emotional sensitivity will be fostered during this difficult 'in-between' period of adolescent development.

Such pre-parental preparation is therefore likely to be a promising way of influencing young people before firm attitudes towards their own children are established. It must additionally be accompanied by extensive practical experience with real babies and children. The importance of the school years lies in the fact that they are the only period during which all prospective parents can be reached since pupils are a 'captive population'.

Subsequently similar experiences should be offered to young adults in a variety of settings, continuing into what may well turn out to be the most impressionable period, namely pregnancy and early parenthood. Neighbourhood schemes, wherever possible including home-based guidance and support, in which couples are actively involved rather than 'lectured at', are likely to stand the best chance of attracting interest and of modifying parental attitudes and behaviour.

There seems to be now an increasing interest in the possibilities of developing flexible schemes of preparing young people for parent-hood as well as offering a varied range of support services during the early years of parenthood. A recent review of current initiatives shows that a considerable number of parents, drawn from all walks of life, are participating in such schemes. However, a great many have at present no opportunity to do so, particularly those with very young children (Pugh, 1980).

If done well and if appropriately supported by the media – television, radio, women's magazines, etc. – then preparation for parenthood would achieve a number of aims, all of which would ensure better and more enjoyable parenting. It would make explicit why love alone is not enough for successfully promoting the helpless baby's potentialities for emotional, intellectual and physical develop-ment to the fullest, particularly during the vital early years of growth.

Making clear why mothering (or fathering for that matter) is among the world's most important, creative jobs – if also among the most difficult to do well – would raise its status and confer equality of esteem in the eyes of both men and women upon those mothers who choose to devote themselves full-time to the rearing of the future generation. (That adequate financial, housing and other kinds of support are prerequisites to enable women to make this choice without suffering severe economic hardship goes without saying.)

Women may then come to be freed from the multiple yokes which current mythology, social pressures and poverty have fastened upon them: mothers of under-fives who have continued to withstand the pressures on them to seek outside employment – and they are still the vast majority – would no longer be almost forced to apologise for their choice (and for enjoying it) and to suffer nevertheless a sense of low esteem and inadequacy for 'not working'; they would on the contrary receive social approval for getting their priorities right.

Those who are at present combining child-rearing with paid employment would no longer be brainwashed to consider that leading guilt-ridden, overworked dual lives is either in their own interest or in that of their children. Those who decide that they wish to fulfil their creative talents in ways other than child-rearing would be respected for making a responsible choice; much more responsible than those who succumb to the present dangerous dogma which seeks to turn women into mere 'breeding machines' by liberating them from all but pregnancy and labour at the price of sacrificing young children's need for individual mothering.

How can professionals be prepared to share power with parents?

If responsible and confident parenthood is to be encouraged, then parental involvement must not only be welcomed but actively fostered. Accepting parents as full partners does not come easily to professionals whose training continues to be based on the traditional model of the authoritative, knowledgeable and skilled expert whose role is to diagnose, treat or teach, doing things to and for rather than with the patient/client/student. For example, in the education system, how children are taught, what they are expected to learn, whether or not they are subjected to corporal punishment, whether or not they are ready for full-time schooling at the age of five years – in relation to none of these issues are parents' wishes and views either ascertained or taken into account.

To begin with, preparing professional workers to share power with parents should become part of their basic training as well as of refresher courses for experienced practitioners. Secondly, successful schemes where such partnership has become well established, should be widely publicised and the way in which the schemes are organised should be evaluated and disseminated. The work of pre-school playgroups is one example and some specially devised support services for families with handicapped children is another (Pugh and Russell, 1977).

A third, rather different circumstance could be deliberately used as an incentive, namely the reality of resource constraints. These could be turned to advantage since by promoting parental involvement, available skilled manpower could be used more effectively; also parents can become very powerful pressure groups for meeting the needs of children when allied to the expertise and know-how of the professional establishment.

Should different services and professionals pool resources?

No single department of local or central government, and no single profession has 'the key' either to promoting children's all-round development, or to providing solutions to disadvantage and deprivation. The key will be found only through interdepartmental, interdisciplinary co-operation. This surely makes the pooling of knowledge, skills and resources an essential prerequisite. Community resources – voluntary workers of all ages, self-help organisations and the whole range of voluntary bodies – must be included in this collaboration. In laying the basis for such a collaborative philosophy and practice, professional training clearly will have to play a central part.

At present, there is virtually no overall co-ordination of policies or practices in the services provided for children by local or central government. Administrative divisions are exacerbated by professional demarcations and jealousies which form barriers to communication about and a concerted approach to common problems.

The Central Policy Review Staff had this to say in a recent report (1978):

> The real question is whether the government's existing role is sufficient, given the intrinsic importance of ensuring that young children in our society have adequate attention paid to their needs . . . There are four aspects of the services for children where existing policies are inadequate: (a) there is a lack of direction and no clear priorities as to the ways in which services should progress; (b) there is confusion in the administration of services for children under five. The provision of services is fragmented and responsibility divided; (c) the consequences of the present situation for the children and their parents are both unjust and inequitable. There is a serious lost opportunity for preventative work at an early stage; (d) it is widely recognised that children benefit from some education and care outside their homes between the ages of three to five. A substantial number of children are denied this benefit because adequate provision is not available.

If services and professionals are to pool resources, then planning, and in particular the selection of priorities, must go 'across the board', including social, health, education and environmental services (such as housing, transport, etc.). Corporate planning has now become an accepted principle at local government level, if not yet a fully worked out procedure. A beginning has been made too with setting up joint planning teams and with establishing joint financing arrangements.

There is a strong case for creating further joint planning teams.

Perhaps the most suitable areas to begin with are assessment services, provision for the under-fives and intermediate treatment facilities, all of which already involve participation by more than one profession and department. Family planning and preparation for parenthood are two other areas with great potential for joint planning and co-operation at field-work level.

Operational co-ordination across not only departmental but agency boundaries could facilitate a fuller use of existing facilities. Examples are the use of nursery schools by those attending day nurseries; the use of playgroups by child-minders; of sports facilities belonging to schools and universities by intermediate treatment projects; of community homes for training mothers in child care; and so on.

Once the areas for co-operation have been identified it would, of course, be up to the local authorities and local planning groups to choose the options most suited to local needs. This may necessitate a greater flexibility in making grants from central to local government. Also, services vary widely from one part of the country to another in both quality and quantity. It would help to raise standards if central government were to issue guidelines about desirable minimum standards, at least for those services where the local authority stands *in loco parentis*.

Prevention – impossible dream or essential reality?

Too often it is judged more urgent or more feasible to consider the relative costs of different policies – in terms of taxpayers' money, not psychological effects – rather than the kind of children or adults we are creating and the kind we want. Instead, it might be helpful to spell out those aims or goals of child-care policies on which there is probably a broad consensus. They can be summarised under three general headings:

The first is to promote the physical development of children. This must involve much more than simple survival and the prevention of handicap; it must be concerned with the quality of life, the promotion of physical vitality and the whole range of motor skills.

The second goal is to promote the psychological development of children, which covers an even wider range of skills, behaviour and qualities. Among them are language and communication; resourcefulness and coping strategies; intellectual growth and scholastic attainments; and, above all, the capacity for caring and sharing, for developing emotional attachment, warmth, trust and a willingness to help others. Perhaps the term which best summarises the aims of psychological development is 'overall competence' which is reflected in all the child's behaviour – relations with other people, the use and understanding of language, knowledge of social situations and involvement in creative activities.

The third goal is to provide children with a pleasant childhood, free from hunger and pain, insecurity and fear, pressure and stress, abuse and neglect. This aim is seldom made explicit in policy statements – perhaps because it seems obvious or is thought to be too 'unscientific'. It nevertheless deserves mention because it is the hallmark of a civilised society that childhood is treated as an important period for its own sake and not merely as a preparation for adulthood.

The second and third aims are inter-related. Perhaps the puritanical ethic has held sway for too long, on the mistaken assumption that happiness and high standards are mutually incompatible. Enlightened common sense has rather satisfyingly received valuable support from recent research which shows that academic achievement in socially deprived areas is far more influenced by the ethos, positive values and encouragement given by the school, and by the personal example and attitudes of the teachers, rather than by such aspects as the age of the buildings, the size of the school or the amount of punishment (Rutter *et al.*, 1979).

Happiness and academic achievements are thus seen to be not alternatives but to go together. If this is so for adolescents, then it is bound to be the case to an even greater extent in the far closer relationships between parents and children: it is neither income, social position nor severity of discipline, but the loving care, personal example and positive encouragement given by parents which promote happy as well as capable children. In short, it is the loved baby who in turn becomes the loving adult.

If these aims are to be met, prevention must involve the framing of policies to deal with a number of basic issues: how to encourage and support 'good' parenting; when and how to identify children 'at risk' so as to mitigate the effects of handicap or of neglect, deprivation and ill-treatment; how to intervene for the sake of the child's safety and happiness; and how to improve the care of children growing up apart from their biological families. To translate them into practice and to make prevention an essential reality will require changes of attitudes.

To begin with, a truly child-centred approach would have to be adopted. This means that we must be more willing to listen to the voices of children themselves and become more skilled in interpreting them. Even toddlers reveal by their behaviour and through their play whether their need for loving, consistent care is being met or not.

Next, all professional workers would have to become much more aware of, and sensitive to, the early warning signals which are invariably shown by children whose basic psychological needs are not being adequately met. These 'signals' might be called 'multidisciplinary indicators'. Chief among them are failure to thrive physically despite apparently adequate nutrition; difficulties in relationships with adults or other children, whether of an aggressive or withdrawn nature; disturbances of behaviour or habits such as sleeping or eating; developmental lag, whether in language or educational achievements; or marked regression to more immature forms of coping. Only if all the professional workers involved acquire a sound grounding in normal child development, as well as first-hand experience of working with children, can the necessary understanding of, and alertness to, such indicators be developed.

Lastly, a continuous watching brief would have to be held over those children who are at special risk of emotional neglect and rejection, as well as of physical ill-treatment. This seems an essential safeguard. It is also now a practical possibility since much is known about the major family, personal and social conditions which indicate the likelihood of such risks.

The way forward

There is a tendency in this country to belittle our achievements and to compare ourselves unfavourably with other nations. To some extent most of the contributors to this book, including myself, may have shown this characteristic. Such an attitude leads to the danger of talking ourselves into a mood of unjustified gloom and defeatism. In fact, there are substantial grounds for hope and optimism. For one thing, rather than being 'the sick man' of Europe, as both academic economists and the media claim, a careful American analyst comes to the opposite conclusion.

In the first thirty years after World War II, Britain enjoyed the fastest rate of economic growth in its recorded history . . . This unprecedented growth has transformed the living standards of ordinary people. When the Queen celebrated her Silver Jubilee in 1977, each of her subjects on average enjoyed incomes commanding almost four-fifths more in goods and services than their parents. Even allowing for the great rise in prices, 'real' and not inflated incomes after taxes had grown by 88 per cent between 1952 and 1976. (Nossiter, 1978)

The author goes on to demonstrate that similar improvements were shown by a host of other indicators such as health, infant mortality, the life expectation of men and women, the proportion of people who have an indoor lavatory, a bath, a car and a television set. Moreover, 'the rising tide of prosperity had lifted the poor as well as the rich. The number living below the poverty line fell from one-fifth of the population in 1953–4 to one-fortieth in 1973, an eightfold gain . . . Britons got richer; their neighbours got richer faster. That is the hard core of fact in the layers of gloom produced in the popular pulpits.'

Having offered such a hopeful and positive analysis of the past, Nossiter then turns to an examination of this slower growth rate and concludes that Britons value leisure more highly than goods. He presents evidence to show that both workers and businessmen alike prefer a slower-paced, uncompetitive and unaggressive life, appearing to be 'satisfying rather than optimising. Workers and managers do not seek the greatest possible income; they seek instead an adequate or satisfactory level of income. They prefer tea breaks and long executive lunches, slower assembly lines and longer week-ends to strenuous effort for higher incomes.' Of course, Nossiter recognises that this outlook does not apply to the fortunate minority for whom work is an enjoyable, rewarding, creative form of self-expression. 'The preference for leisure over goods applies chiefly to those toiling in mines or assembly lines, labouring at routine tasks in huge white-collar bureaucracies, public and private.'

The question why this preference should have occurred in Britain before any other industrial country is as difficult to answer as why the Industrial Revolution came here first. Thus Nossiter sees Britain as 'a solid, healthy society bursting with creative vigour'. As evidence he cites the fact that even in as difficult a year as 1974, over 84 per cent of all male and over 89 per cent of female workers declared themselves as 'satisfied' with their jobs (Central Statistical Office, 1976). 'This is not the response of a sullen, class-ridden, divided nation', he argues. Rather, 'post-industrial Britain semi-consciously practises a new and more lasting empire of the spirit, quietly insinuating the values it proclaims (and frequently practises) – tolerance, decency, respect for the human personality.'

If Nossiter's analysis is correct – and I for one find it convincing – then it is perhaps justified to hope that just as this country has pioneered the belief that society has a responsibility for its more vulnerable members, so we shall develop an increasing respect for the needs and rights of the most vulnerable yet most promising members of our society – our children.

Grounds for hope and optimism can also be found in a recent example of how much can be achieved by determined, sustained and effective co-operation. The spectacular success of space exploration has proved that problems of incredible complexity can be solved. It has shown, too, that scientists and practitioners from a whole spectrum of disciplines can work together, transcending their professional boundaries. As I see it, the biggest achievement of the space programme lies in the fact that such a feat of collaborative thought and action, involving many thousands of individuals, proved to be attainable. The spur was a goal judged to be sufficiently important and a challenge sufficiently exciting, backed by all the necessary financial support and scientific expertise.

Surely to create a more compassionate, caring society is an equally, if not more important, goal? And is not the aim of reconciling personal fulfilment and freedom with the individual's obligations and commitment to the needs of his community a sufficiently exciting challenge? Ought we not to will the means to improve in this way the quality of life for all our children, the seedcorn of tomorrow?

Bibliography

Clarke-Stewart, A. (1977) *Child Care in the Family* (New York: Academic Press).

Central Policy Review Staff (1978) *Services for Working Mothers with Young Children* (London: HMSO).

Central Statistical Office (1976) *Social Trends*, no. 7 (London: HMSO).

Fogelman, K. (ed.) (1976) *Britain's Sixteen-Year-Olds* (London: National Children's Bureau).

Kamerman, S. B. and Kahn, A. J. (eds) (1978) *Family Policy: Government and Families in Fourteen Countries* (New York: Columbia University Press).

National Research Council (1976) *Toward a National Policy for Children and Families* (Washington: National Academy of Sciences).

Newsam, P. A. (1979) Address to the Annual Meeting of the Secondary Head Teachers Association (available from ILEA).

Nossiter, B. D. (1978) *Britain – a Future that Works* (London: André Deutsch).

Page, R. and Clark, G. A. (eds) (1977) *Who Cares? Young People in Care Speak Out* (London: National Children's Bureau).

Parker, H. (1978) *Who Pays for the Children?* (London: The Outer Circle Policy Unit).

Pilling, D. and Pringle, M. K. (1978) *Controversial Issues in Child Development* (London: Elek).

Pringle, M. K. (ed.) (1965) *Investment in Children* (London: Longman).

Pringle, M. K. (1980) *The Needs of Children*, 2nd edn (London: Hutchinson).

Pugh, G. (1980) (ed.) 'Preparation for Parenthood: some Current Initiatives and Thinking' (London: National Children's Bureau).

Pugh, G. and Russell, P. (1977) *Shared Care: Support Services for Families with Handicapped Children* (London: National Children's Bureau).

Rodgers, B. (1976) 'A view from abroad', *Concern*, no. 22, pp. 7–12.

Rutter, M. Maughan, B., Mortimore, P., Ouston, J. and Smith, A. (1979) *Fifteen Thousand Hours: Secondary Schools and Their Effects on Children* (London: Open Books).

Walley, J. (1972) *Social Security: Another British Failure?* (London: Charles Knight).

Weber, C. U., Foster, P. W. and Weikart, D. P. (1978). *An Economic Analysis of the Ypsilanti Perry Preschool Project* (Ypsilanti, Michigan: High/Scope Educational Research Foundation).

Wedge, P. and Prosser, H. (1973). *Born to Fail?* (London: Arrow Books).

Weikart, D. P., Epstein, A. S., Schweinhart, L. and Bond, J. T. (1978) *The Ypsilanti Preschool Curriculum Demonstration Project: Preschool Years and Longitudinal Results.* (Ypsilanti, Michigan: High/Scope Educational Research Foundation).

Index